5

CONCISE COLLEGE TEXT

THE ENGLISH
LEGAL SYSTEM

AUSTRALIA AND NEW ZEALAND
The Law Book Company Ltd.
Sydney : Melbourne : Perth

CANADA AND U.S.A.
The Carswell Company Ltd.
Agincourt, Ontario

INDIA
N. M. Tripathi Private Ltd.
Bombay
and
Eastern Law House Private Ltd.
Calcutta and Delhi
M.P.P. House
Bangalore

ISRAEL
Steimatzky's Agency Ltd.
Jerusalem : Tel Aviv : Haifa

MALAYSIA : SINGAPORE : BRUNEI
Malayan Law Journal (Pte.) Ltd.
Singapore and Kuala Lumpur

PAKISTAN
Pakistan Law House
Karachi

CONCISE COLLEGE TEXTS

THE ENGLISH LEGAL SYSTEM

By

KEITH J. EDDEY B.A.(HONS.), B.LITT.,
Solicitor

FOURTH EDITION

LONDON • SWEET & MAXWELL • 1987

First Published 1971
Second Edition 1977
Third Edition 1982
Fourth Edition 1987

Published in 1987 by
Sweet & Maxwell Limited of
11 New Fetter Lane, London.
Computerset by Promenade Graphics Limited, Cheltenham
Reproduced, printed and bound in Great Britain by
Hazell Watson & Viney Limited,
Member of the BPCC Group,
Aylesbury, Bucks

British Library Cataloguing in Publication Data
   Eddey, K. J.
      The English legal system.—4th ed.—
      (Concise college texts)
      1. Law—England 2. Justice
      Administration of—England
      I. Title   II. Series
      344.207   KD660

      ISBN 0–421–35400–3
      ISBN 0–421–35410–0 Pbk

Preface

The purpose of this book remains that of providing students with a straightforward introduction to the English Legal System.

The emphasis, as in previous editions, is on the contemporary nature of the system with illustrations taken from recent statutes, cases, statistics and annual reports.

Like the substantive law the Legal System is subject to change and this has been especially borne out in the current revision of the text. Amendments have been called for in most chapters, particularly in those relating to the Legal Profession, the Courts, Tribunals, Legal Aid and Procedure and Evidence.

Pending legislation includes a major Criminal Justice Bill, whilst changes are expected in the relationship between the two branches of the legal profession, in civil procedure, in legal aid and advice provision and, perhaps, in the establishment of a Family Court.

I remain grateful to my publishers for their help and efficiency and to my wife for her continued interest and assistance.

Cumnor, Oxford,
November 1986

Keith J. Eddey

Contents

Table of Cases

Table of Statutes

1. The Legal Profession

1. Barristers and Solicitors

In the English legal system a practising lawyer must hold one of two professional qualifications; he must either have been admitted to practise as a solicitor or have been called to the Bar as a barrister. This division of the legal profession is of long standing and each branch has its own characteristic functions as well as a separate governing body.

The barrister is usually thought of primarily as an advocate, since this is the work in which he is most often engaged. He has the virtually exclusive right of audience as an advocate before all the superior courts, and he can also take cases in the inferior courts if he wishes to do so. When acting professionally barristers are known as "counsel." In total there are, at the last count, 5,367 barristers in practice, a number which is just about small enough to make this branch of the profession a closely-knit unit. One result of this factor, as will be seen in the next chapter, is that the senior judges in the English legal system are drawn exclusively from the ranks of experienced counsel.

The solicitor can be an advocate in the inferior courts but he is more familiar to the public in his role as a general legal adviser. There are approximately 46,490 solicitors in practice and their offices are a familiar feature in the business centres of cities and towns throughout England and Wales.

A significant difference between the two professions is that members of the public are able to call at a solicitor's office and seek his advice in a personal interview; whereas a barrister can at present only be consulted indirectly through a solicitor. It can be seen that there is a possible analogy in these circumstances to the medical profession, with the solicitor being regarded as a general practitioner and the barrister as a consultant. The analogy must not be taken too far however, since the legal knowledge of the newly qualified barris-

1

ter is not to be compared with that of the senior partners of a firm of solicitors, whose legal experience may extend over many years and cover diverse fields of law. In many instances too the solicitor is more of a specialist than the barrister, particularly where the latter is an advocate with a common law practice.

Apart from the barristers and solicitors who are involved in the private practice of the law, it is necessary to remember that a large number of professionally qualified lawyers are employed in central and local government, in commerce and industry and in education. Many of these, because they are not engaged in the practice of the law, would not be included in the figures given above.

Recent legislation, the Administration of Justice Act 1985, looks likely to bring into being a new profession of licensed conveyancers, which includes solicitors and legal executives as well as persons who prove to a conveyancing committee, by examination, that they are competent to transfer property. Such persons are not of course able to practise in any other way as solicitors or barristers.

2. Training

(i) Barristers

A would-be barrister must first register as a student member of one of the four Inns of Court. The Inns of Court are Gray's Inn, Lincoln's Inn, Inner Temple and Middle Temple. All these institutions are to be found in close proximity to the Royal Courts of Justice in London. These four establishments, to one of which every barrister and judge must belong, have a long history as the original homes of the earliest advocates to practise as a profession.

Detailed regulations govern entry to the profession. The general pattern is for the student to obtain a law degree and thereafter to undergo vocational training known as the practical exercises. This training is provided by the Council of Legal Education operating on behalf of the Senate of the Inns of Court. On satisfactory completion of the vocational course the student is called to the Bar by his Inn of Court. Students who do not have a law degree have to take and pass a group of examinations in law subjects before proceeding to the vocational course. Whilst studying to become a barrister the student is required to attend his Inn of Court to obtain an awareness of the ways of the profession which he is intending to join. His attendance is enforced by the requirement that he is present for a number of dinners each legal term.

Even after his call to the Bar the student's training is not, at present, complete, because if he intends to practise as a barrister he has to undergo a process known as pupillage. This involves his understudying a junior counsel in his day to day practice for a period of 12 months. To balance the picture it is necessary to stress that many individuals who qualify as barristers do not intend to enter practice after their call; this is especially so in the case of many students from overseas. No pupillage requirement applies to these students.

(ii) Solicitors

Training for the would-be solicitor has long been a combination of examinations in law, and the understudying of a solicitor in practice. This latter process involves the student in spending a period of time as an articled clerk.

The usual method of entry is by the student obtaining a law degree and then proceeding to a series of vocational examinations set by the Law Society. However provision is made for non-law graduates and mature staff to qualify as solicitors by undergoing an educational stage to be completed before the vocational stage can be attempted. For all students a period in articles will be compulsory.

When the student has completed his articles satisfactorily, and passed all the examinations to which he is subject, he may then apply to the Law Society to be "admitted." This process is effected by the Master of the Rolls formally adding the name of the new solicitor to the roll of officers of the Supreme Court. From the date of admission the student becomes a solicitor of the Supreme Court and as such an officer of the court, but he may not practise until he has taken out an annual practising certificate individually issued by the Law Society. There is a substantial annual fee payable to the Law Society for the practising certificate and an additional payment to the compensation fund is also required. This is the fund from which payments are made by the Law Society to clients who have suffered financial loss through the misconduct of a solicitor. In order to obtain his practising certificate the solicitor also has to comply with very detailed regulations governing solicitors' accounts and pay a substantial annual premium through the Law Society for indemnity insurance against negligence claims.

3. Organisation

The organisation of the two branches of the legal profession is the responsibility of two quite independent governing bodies.

Barristers
(i) **The Inns of Court.** The four Inns of Court are administered by their respective senior members who are called the Benchers. As the

Inn of Court which registers the student is also responsible for calling him to the Bar and supervising his professional life thereafter, even having the power to disbar him, it is obvious that some joint consultation by the Inns of Court is necessary.

(ii) The Senate. This consultation is provided by the Senate of the Inns of Court and the Bar which is made up of the Attorney-General, the Solicitor-General, the Chairman of the Council of Legal Education, 24 Bench Representatives, 12 Hall Representatives, 39 Bar Representatives elected by the Bar, 3 circuit judges, 1 representative of minor judicial offices, 4 officers elected by the Senate and not more than 12 additional members. The Senate now controls the admission and call arrangements for students and also exercises the Inns of Court's disciplinary powers over barristers. Although the Inn of Court still imposes the punishment, its finding is automatic following the Senate's decision. The most serious punishment is, of course, for the barrister to be disbarred. There is no statutory provision, as in the case of solicitors, for the regulation of barristers. The power appears to derive at common law from the judges and has been transferred, with their implied consent, to the Inns of Court and now to the Senate.

(iii) The Bar Council. This is the body which represents all barristers and which in some senses is the non-statutory equivalent of the Law Society. Set up in 1894 it receives financial support from the Inns of Court and from individual barristers. It is perhaps best regarded as "the voice of the Bar," and thus acts in relation to remuneration and conditions of service and professional etiquette, like a barristers' trade union. It does not exercise disciplinary powers and many of its former functions have been transferred to the Senate.

(iv) The Council of Legal Education. As the name indicates this body deals with the arrangements for the admission, examination and training of students in their preparation for call to the Bar. It is controlled by the Senate and employs its own lecturing and administrative staff.

(v) Junior Counsel and Queen's Counsel. All practising barristers are junior counsel unless they have been designated Queen's Counsel (Q.C.). There are some 545 Queen's Counsel in practice. The status is bestowed on about 45 counsel a year by the Queen on the advice of the Lord Chancellor. Annually, the Lord Chancellor's office issues an invitation to junior counsel, who may wish to be considered for designation, to apply. Before a junior counsel can hope to achieve the status he must be able to point to at least 10 years' successful practice as a barrister. The strange system of inviting applications results from the fact that the change of status is, financially, something of a speculation. Once appointed, the Queen's Counsel is barred from much routine work and is expected to appear only in the most important cases, for which briefs may not be so readily available. He is known as a "Leader" presumably because by long standing tradition he is usually accompanied in a court case by one, and sometimes two, junior counsel. The process of becoming a Queen's Counsel is called "taking silk," referring to the fact that the new status involves a change from a stuff gown to a silk gown.

(vi) The Barrister's Clerk. Just as solicitors have their legal executives, so it is common practice for a group of barristers in chambers to share a clerk. In both instances the persons concerned play a major part in the practice and it is said that his clerk can make, or break, the barrister. The barrister's clerk arranges the work of the barrister and negotiates the fee to be marked on the brief by the solicitor unless it is a legal aid case when the taxing officer of the court will assess the fee. There is a Barristers' Clerks' Association which operates a training scheme for admission to the Association.

Solicitors
(i) The Law Society. Solicitors are subject to the Law Society which operates from the Law Society's Hall in Chancery Lane in London. The Society is controlled by an elected body consisting of a Counsel and an annually elected President, and they are assisted by a full-time Secretary and a large Secretariat. The Law Society is recognised for certain purposes in Acts of Parliament and in this way it has control over all solicitors. For other non-statutory purposes membership of the Law Society is voluntary. The Society publishes the *Law Society's Gazette* for its voluntary members and makes other facilities, such as accommodation, available. For disciplinary purposes over the profession Parliament has arranged for the establishment of a Solicitors' Disciplinary Tribunal which deals with alleged professional misconduct by solicitors. This Tribunal is made up of solicitors and lay members appointed by the Master of the Rolls. A quorum is three and the Tribunal has power to strike the name of the offending solicitor off the Rolls, or they may suspend a solicitor from practice, reprimand him, order him to pay a penalty to the Crown of up to £3,000 or order him to pay certain costs. Appeal against these findings lies to the Queen's Bench Divisional Court

and from that court with leave to the Court of Appeal (Civil Division) and possibly even to the House of Lords. Special statutory provisions deal with the employment by solicitors of former solicitors or clerks, who have been dealt with by the Disciplinary Tribunal or by the courts, for offences which would make it undesirable for them to be further employed in legal practice.

(ii) The British Legal Association. In addition to the Law Society there is in existence a British Legal Association. This is intended to be a more active pressure group on behalf of solicitors, and one which will be free of what the Association sees as the inhibitions of the Law Society, with its rather complex statutory and non-statutory basis. It has a current membership of approximately 2,000.

(iii) The Institute of Legal Executives. The body which represents the senior persons employed in solicitors' offices is the Institute of Legal Executives. This organisation replaced the former Managing Clerks' Association and now has its own publication, and its own examination system for admission as an Associate or a Fellow of the Institute. The routine work of a solicitor's office is largely carried out by Legal Executives, and they make an important contribution to the general effectiveness of legal practice.

(iv) The Lay Observer. This office was created to provide a lay voice in the investigation of complaints against solicitors. The Lay Observer publishes an annual report dealing with the complaints received and the action taken. His influence with the Law Society has improved the way in which complaints are investigated and dealt with.

4. History

The division of the legal profession into advocates on the one hand, and those who prepare the case for the advocate on the other hand, has been traced back to about 1340.

The barristers seem to have been known originally as "apprentices-at-law," and those who were given the right of audience before the senior law courts were known as serjeants-at-law. This rank was abolished by one of the provisions of the Judicature Act 1873.

Those who were concerned with the paper work preparation of legal cases were called "attorneys" in the common law courts, "proctors" in the ecclesiastical and admiralty courts and "solicitors" in the chancery courts. As the Inns of Court developed their exclusiveness in the field of advocacy in the sixteenth century, so in 1739 an organisation was set up called "The Society of Gentlemen Practisers in the courts of Law and Equity," which grouped together the non-advocates. It was this same society which ultimately was to give way to the Law Society, incorporated in 1831 and granted a royal charter in 1845. At the same time the term "solicitor" came to be the accepted description for the non-barrister lawyer, as the term "barrister" also became accepted as the descriptive term for the professional advocate.

5. Work of Barristers and Solicitors

(i) Barristers

Most barristers are professional advocates earning their living by the presentation of civil and criminal cases in court. As such, a barrister must be capable of prosecuting in a criminal case one day, and defending an accused person the next; or of preparing the pleadings and taking the case for a plaintiff in a civil action one day, and doing the same for a defendant the next. In this way the barrister attains a real degree of objectivity and of independence of mind. He becomes a specialist at advocacy.

At the same time it is a mistake to regard the barrister entirely as an advocate. In practice there is a great deal of paper work involved in the pre-trial stages of a case, particularly so where a civil action is in question and pleadings have to be prepared. Again barristers will often be asked to give written advice on a particular legal matter without there needing to be any likelihood of an actual case following; this is known as "taking counsel's opinion." So it can be said that all barristers do spend a lot of time at paper work apart from their actual appearances in court in their capacity as advocates. Indeed some barristers who have specialised in a particular branch of the law as, for example, planning law, tax law or employment law, may do most of their work from their rooms or chambers in documentary form and only occasionally appear in the courts as advocates.

Three out of four practising barristers work in London. The remainder operate from one of some thirty provincial centres.

Barristers are not allowed to form partnerships, but may share the same set of chambers and also frequently share a clerk, so that there are very close links between them. By the very way in which their work comes to hand, it often happens that cases overlap or are fixed for the same day, and then another barrister has to take the case at short notice. In such instances the chamber system does prove useful. The ability to grasp the point of a case quickly and the adaptability to move from court to court, and case to case, at short notice is the mark of the experienced barrister.

The remuneration of a barrister is negotiated on his behalf by his clerk and the fee is then marked on the brief, *i.e.* the instructions in the case. Because of an ancient theory that the barrister is giving his services he is not able in law to sue for his fees.

(ii) Solicitors

The name-plates of firms of solicitors are an everyday sight in cities and towns in England and Wales; and although a one-man practice is by no means rare—currently about one in three firms—the trend is towards having several solicitors in partnership. This gives them the opportunity to specialise to some extent, so that whilst one partner may spend all his time on conveyancing, another will deal with litigation, another with probate and trusts and so on. In some of the larger London firms there are more than 20 partners and this means that each can really specialise in a branch of the law in which he has an interest.

The estimated 6,700 firms of solicitors in England and Wales will deal with whatever legal problems are brought to them by members of the public and this means that there is no end to the variety of matters which can appear on a solicitor's desk. A great deal of time is devoted to the transfer of property, whether by way of sale or lease, and this particular skill is known as conveyancing. A solicitor, acting for a client who is selling property, guarantees that he will transfer the legal title to the property effectively and will obtain and pay to the client the purchase money which the client has agreed to accept. A solicitor acting for a purchaser guarantees that the client is getting a valid legal title to the property which he has agreed to buy. A statutory Conveyancing Council, established by the Administration of Justice Act 1985, exists to license and supervise persons who wish to practise as conveyancers. This development has abolished the monopoly formerly enjoyed by solicitors in conveyancing. The Law Society administers a contribution fund, which is available to compensate any person who suffers financial loss as a result of dishonest conduct on the part of a solicitor in the course of his professional obligations. Solicitors may also be sued in the courts for negligence by a client, who alleges that his solicitor is in breach of his duty to take proper care in the handling of the client's particular matter.

Besides conveyancing, a solicitor's practice will usually extend to probate work, which is concerned with the obtaining of legal title to a deceased person's estate and then with the actual winding up and distribution of that estate. Litigation, including divorce, is a fruitful source of work for a large number of solicitors since, as has been seen, the solicitor is responsible for preparing the whole of the case, and the barrister receives this in the form of a brief from which he plans his advocacy in the particular case. Since litigation extends from the lowest county court to the largest High Court claim, and from minor summary to major indictable criminal offences, it can readily be grasped that solicitors behind the scenes have a major role in this vitally important branch of the law. Nor should it be overlooked that solicitors have a right of audience as advocates in the county court, in magistrates' courts and, for certain cases, in the Crown Court and the High Court.

These three fields of activity—conveyancing, probate and litigation—are those which come most readily to mind but there is no limit to the topics involving legal considerations which may find their way to a solicitor's office. Tax law, company law, the activities of local authorities in such matters as compulsory purchase, highway maintenance and improvement and in planning decisions, with all these legal matters and a host of others too, solicitors are from time to time involved.

The remuneration of solicitors is to some extent controlled. In litigation the costs claimed by the solicitors are examined—or more correctly "taxed"—by the appropriate officer of the court concerned. This is known as "contentious business." Even where solicitors are engaged in "non-contentious business" the costs are still controlled in the sense that whilst there is no longer a fixed scale of costs the charge made must be fair and reasonable having regard to all the circumstances of the case. For details reference should be made to the Solicitors' Remuneration Order 1972. It is possible for a client to challenge a charge by forcing the solicitor to obtain a certificate from the Law Society to the effect that the charge is fair and reasonable. Finally it is to be noted that a solicitor, unlike a barrister, can sue for his fees in an ordinary court action.

6. Professional Etiquette

Both barristers and solicitors are closely restricted in their professional conduct by the supervision of their respective governing bodies. The former rigorous prohibition on advertising has been relaxed sufficiently to enable a solicitor to advertise the work he does, and in conveyancing the charges which he makes. Barristers remain precluded from advertising. At the time of writing the restrictive practices which require a barrister to take instructions only through a solicitor and which give barristers a virtually exclusive right of audience in the superior courts are both under consideration. Currently a barrister only meets the lay client when the solicitor, or his representative, is present; so building up the isolation, as well as the objectivity, of the barrister. In order to prevent barristers gaining unfair advantage by cultivating the friendship of solicitors, there used to be a rule which prevented a solicitor and a barrister in a case from having lunch together. Solicitors are likewise under a professional duty not to entice another solicitor's clients away from him.

Barristers and solicitors are required to dress formally when appearing in a court case; for a barrister this involves wearing wig and gown, since without these he cannot be "seen" or "heard" by the judge. Solicitors appearing in the county, Crown or High Court must wear a gown but no wig.

Although solicitors have long been able to form partnerships, the barrister is not permitted to share his responsibilities in this way. He does have the benefit of contact with other barristers in the chambers of which he is a member, but he remains an independent unit, standing or falling entirely by his own efforts. By professional tradition the fees of a barrister are a gratuity—it is said that the gown of a barrister still has a pocket to receive this "present"—so that he cannot sue for fees earned. In practice, however, solicitors are responsible for these fees, and as such the Law Society regards it as a professional obligation for solicitors, even if themselves unpaid, to settle the fees of a barrister whom they have instructed.

A longstanding principle, which was confirmed by the House of Lords decision in *Rondel* v. *Worsley* (1969) is that a barrister cannot be sued for negligence whilst acting as an advocate. In *Saif Ali* v. *Sydney Mitchell and Co.* [1978] a barrister was found to have been negligent in pre-trial advice and it was held that he was not entitled to immunity. A solicitor can be sued for negligence, although he probably has the same immunity as a barrister when acting as an advocate.

Barristers, as a matter of etiquette, refer to each other in court as "my learned friend"; they do not make a habit of shaking hands with each other; and they do not use headed notepaper. Solicitors are kept informed of the opinions of the Law Society, which they are expected to observe, as well as the various statutory matters which bind them. These latter extend from the annual payments for the practising certificate and to the contribution fund, to the strict observance of the solicitors' accounts rules.

Finally, one result of the division of the legal profession is that no one can be both a barrister and a solicitor at the same time. Provision has however been made for transfer from one profession to the other.

7. Change and the Legal Profession

The past 20 years have increasingly shown that lawyers are not insulated from change. First the Ormrod Committee, which reported in 1971, critically examined the training of lawyers and recommended substantial alterations with a common academic stage to be followed by vocational training. Many of the proposals have been implemented.

Critical attention was then directed to the provision of Legal Services by a Royal Commission (Chairman Lord Benson) which reported in 1979. Contrary to expectations the report revealed general satisfaction with the current position. It came out against the suggested "fusion" of the legal profession, finding that the existing division ensured the highest standard of advocacy and best served the public interest. Its many recommendations to improve the provision of legal services frequently called for increased government spending. Predictably these proposals have generally not been implemented.

Nonetheless substantial change has occurred and looks certain to continue. The solicitors' conveyancing monopoly has been broken with substantial adverse consequences for the income of the profession. As a result solicitors are seeking wider rights of audience in litigation so coming into direct conflict with barristers. In turn barristers are questioning the need to have the solicitor present at all interviews with the lay client and challenging the restriction under which a barrister may only be instructed through a solicitor. Voices are being heard once again proposing the fusion of the profession.

The Lord Chancellor, Lord Hailsham, having been forced by the legal profession through legal action in the courts to reconsider the whole subject of legal aid and advice remuneration, has responded with a wide range of proposals aimed at saving time and costs. These proposals include fundamental changes in the rules which have long governed the dual legal profession. Barristers appearing in cases without the solicitor attending; Q.C.'s appearing without Junior Counsel; cases being dealt with on written representations or with short oral presentation; Legal advice centres to replace the work done by solicitors under the Green Form scheme (see p. 110); these and other changes if accepted would transform the nature of the legal profession out of all recognition. Sadly these proposals seem to be solely governed by considerations of saving the government money and with scant regard for the consequences in terms of the quality of the administration of justice.

Other changes affecting the legal profession already introduced include, a national duty solicitor scheme for magistrates' courts (see p. 73); a Crown Prosecution service under which barristers and solicitors will take over prosecutions from the police (see p. 73); and wider rights of audience for solicitors in the High Court in formal and unopposed hearings (see p. 17).

Such is the depth of concern about the future for the legal profession that a committee chaired by Lady Marre has been established by the Law Society and the Bar to provide a considered reaction to all proposals for change.

2. Judges

1. Appointment

The age-old theory, that the monarch is "the fountain of justice," is still nominally effective in the context of the appointment of judges. The courts of law remain the Queen's Courts and the judges remain Her Majesty's judges.

However, change in the monarch's constitutional role has meant that, whereas originally the power of appointment vested in the monarch was entirely personal, at the present time all judicial appointments are made by the monarch on the advice of representatives of the government of the day.

Thus the Lord Chancellor, the Lord Chief Justice, the Master of the Rolls, the President of the Family Division, the Vice-Chancellor, the Lords of Appeal in Ordinary and the Lords Justices of Appeal are all appointed by the Queen on the advice of the Prime Minister. It is an open secret that the Prime Minister, having selected the Lord Chancellor, will consult with him about these appointments, as vacancies occur, before furnishing her advice to the Queen.

The puisne judges of the High Court, circuit judges, recorders, metropolitan and stipendiary magistrates and the vast numbers of lay magistrates are all appointed on the advice of the Lord Chancellor. A qualification to this statement is that for the area of the Duchy of Lancaster recommendations are made by the Chancellor of the Duchy of Lancaster.

The sole qualification for a senior judicial appointment in the English system is practical experience as a barrister. A minimum period of experience is required, increasing from 10 years for a High Court judge, to 15 years for the Appeal Court judges. A study of actual appointments reveals that very much longer experience of practice than that stated is the usual rule. The system of appointing judges from the ranks of practising counsel is in complete contrast to systems elsewhere, where a civil service career as a judge is a common feature. An even greater contrast is with the system in certain American states, where some appointments to judicial offices are made by the process of democratic election by the local electorate— a method which may seem fraught with peril to those familiar with the ways of the elected representative!

Most English judges are male, although there are at present three female High Court judges, Mrs. Justice Booth, Mrs. Justice Butler-Sloss and Mrs. Justice Heilbron. The number of female counsel in practice rises annually and is currently 696. In 1986 five female barristers were appointed Queen's Counsel. It follows that female appointments to the Bench will become increasingly common.

The Courts Act 1971 broke, to a minor extent, the monopoly of the bar in judicial appointments. It allowed solicitors to be appointed as recorders and some 50 appointments have been made. Once a recorder has had three years' experience he can be appointed a circuit judge. So far this has happened to 20 solicitors. It is not at present possible for a solicitor circuit judge to proceed higher up the judicial ladder.

2. Dismissal

(a) History

The security in office of a judge has an interesting history. For centuries appointment and dismissal was personal to the monarch, so that judges held office *"durante bene placito nostro"*—at pleasure. One result of this state of affairs was that decisions, in cases in which the monarch had an interest, tended to be satisfactory from his or her standpoint. The dangers became increasingly apparent in the seventeenth century in the reigns of James I and Charles I, so that in the Commonwealth period, which followed the Civil War and the execution of Charles I, the judges were given security in office whilst of good behaviour. The Restoration of Charles II in 1660 saw a return to the former practice, and it was not until the Act of Settlement was passed in 1700 that it was finally established that judges were not to be dismissible at the pleasure of the Crown. That statute provided that judges were to hold office, *"quamdiu se bene gesserint"*— whilst of good behaviour—and that they were to be removed only following an address to the monarch from both Houses of Parliament requesting dismissal. This provision is now to be found in the Supreme Court Act 1981. This method of dismissal has not been used, since its original enactment in 1700, to remove an English judge; but it appears that one Irish judge was dismissed under similar provisions in 1830.

Academically there are those who argue that there remains a common law power, vested in the monarch, to dismiss a judge for inability or for serious personal misconduct affecting his office. Since there are no examples of the monarch's use of such a power, the argument is entirely theoretical.

(b) Inferior court judges

The provisions requiring an address from both Houses of Parliament before dismissal only apply to the "superior" judges, by which is meant judges of the High Court, the Court of Appeal and the House of Lords.

The statutes which deal with the system of county courts, the Crown Court and the work of the lay magistrates, make provision for the dismissal of judges and magistrates respectively. In the case of the circuit judge or recorder the Lord Chancellor may remove him for incapacity or for misbehaviour, whilst the Lord Chancellor can remove the name of a magistrate from the Commission without showing cause.

In 1983 a circuit judge was removed after being convicted of attempted smuggling.

Lord Hailsham, the Lord Chancellor, in 1986 whilst defending the existing method of making judicial appointments, announced that he was in favour of the establishment of a Complaints Board to advise him about the possible dismissal of a judge. The Lord Chancellor at present appoints or recommends for appointment some 2,500 judicial office holders.

(c) Resignation

The status and salary of judgeship are such that, other than on grounds of ill-health or retirement, resignation has not been a phenomenon to be reckoned with. Consequently the announcement in 1970, that Mr. Justice Fisher at the age of 52 and after only two years' service as a High Court judge, was to give up his judicial office to follow a career in the business world came as a substantial break with convention.

The Supreme Court Act 1981 permits the Lord Chancellor, after consultation with specified members of the judiciary, to declare vacant the office of any judge of High Court or Appeal Court status who is through ill-health no longer capable of carrying on his work and who is incapable of taking the decision to resign.

(d) Retirement

Until Parliament passed the Judicial Pensions Act 1959, judges were appointed for their lifetime unless they chose to give up office. Since that Act new judges of the High Court and the Appeal Courts are required to retire from office on reaching the age of 75. As a pension of half the current annual salary is earned after 15 years of service as a judge, it is possible for most judges to retire on pension well before reaching compulsory retiring age.

Circuit judges must retire at 72, unless the Lord Chancellor invites them to continue until the age of 75.

3. The independence of the Judiciary

The constitutional doctrine of the separation of powers, stated in its best known form by Montesquieu in *"L'Esprit des Lois"* (1748) and translated into action in the constitution of the United States of America, laid great stress on the need for the judiciary to be kept apart from the legislative and executive functions of government. Montesquieu's view was that if there should be, at any time, a combination of the judicial function with the executive or legislative function then tyranny would result.

In the English system judges are made as independent as possible. By a well understood convention judges do not take part in politics, nor do they allow their political sympathies to affect their judgment. A judge cannot, by statute, also be a Member of Parliament, although some judges are appointed after having had political experience. Lord Fraser of Tullybelton was a candidate for a Parliamentary election before becoming a judge in Scotland and ultimately a senior Law Lord. Judges who are made peers in order to carry out the work of the House of Lords as a supreme court of appeal do not, by convention, take part in political controversy. In return, lay peers do not attend hearings of the court, although in law there appears to be nothing to stop them from doing so. Another convention is that members of the House of Commons do not attack a judge on a personal basis except by moving an address for his removal. Instead, criticism is directed at the legal principle laid down in the case. One apparent anomaly, in the attempt to separate judges from political considerations, is that new appointments are made on the recommendation of the Prime Minister, or the Lord Chancellor, both of whom hold political appointments, but perhaps the strangest anomaly in the system is the position of the Lord Chancellor himself. His appointment is a political one and he has consequently no security of tenure; he is the head of a government department and member of the Cabinet, and he plays a major role in the work of the House of Lords as a legislative assembly. Nonetheless, he is guided by the rule that his political activities must be kept completely apart from the judicial responsibilities of his office.

To the end that judges shall be independent the removal of a superior court judge from office is made a difficult process. They thus enjoy considerable security of tenure. The fact that no English judge has yet been removed by the monarch on an address from both Houses of Parliament is proof positive that their security in office is well founded. Equally the substantial salary which is paid annually to High Court and Court of Appeal judges means that there is no financial incentive on promotion, which might tempt a judge to curry favour with the government of the day. Again, as a gesture, the salaries of judges are paid out of the Consolidated Fund and are thus not subject to annual review, although they are none-theless fixed by Parliament.

As a result of the seventeenth century struggle between the monarch and Parliament, the judiciary accepted the constitutional doctrine of the supremacy of Parliament, and consequently no judge will ever refuse to give effect to legislation properly enacted. In return the legal profession is left substantially free to regulate its own affairs and to make rules of court for the purposes of legal process. This was recently evidenced when a meeting of High Court Judges was called to consider to what extent, if at all, solicitors should have a right of audience in the High Court.

Finally, one of the main factors assuring the independence of the judiciary is the experience of practice at the Bar, in the sense that every judge before his appointment will have had many years' experience of presenting criminal and/or civil cases in court based on his own initiative as an advocate. This professional tradition inevitably creates judges of a most independent frame of mind.

4. Constitutional Status

A nice point which has not been finally determined is whether or not judges are "Crown servants." By virtue of their appointment by the monarch, the possibility of their dismissal by the monarch and their formal title as one of Her Majesty's Justices, it would appear that judges are employed by the Crown and as such are, in law, servants of the Crown. On the other hand it is argued that servants are con-trolled by their master, whereas it is well understood that judges will be independent and will on no account take orders from the Crown. All the rules relating to the independence of the judiciary confirm this view.

This academic consideration became of actual consequence in 1931, when, by an order in council made under the National Econ-omy Act 1931, the salaries of all "persons in His Majesty's service" were to be reduced by 10 per cent. The point was taken that this phrase ought not to be interpreted as including the judiciary, but the

Commissioners of Inland Revenue issued orders purporting to reduce judicial salaries nonetheless. Unfortunately, the point was never settled, because circumstances reflecting public opinion led to the withdrawal of the orders.

A contrast can be drawn with colonial judges, who form a part of the civil service and who thus have not the special status, security in office and independence, which is associated with the English judiciary. In *Terrell* v. *Secretary of State for the Colonies* (1953), a colonial judge whose appointment came to a premature end was held to be without remedy, being a Crown servant and dismissible at pleasure.

5. Judicial Immunity

An extension of the principle that the judiciary must be independent is the concept of judicial immunity, which lays down that a judge may not be sued in a civil action for things said or acts done in the exercise of his judicial office.

The precise application of this immunity has, in the past, varied with the status of the judge. Whereas a High Court judge had complete immunity an inferior court judge could claim immunity only when acting within his jurisdiction. Magistrates had even less immunity and might even be liable, if acting maliciously or without reasonable cause, although within their jurisdiction.

In *Sirros* v. *Moore* (1975) the Court of Appeal had to consider the immunity of a circuit judge and Lord Denning M.R. indicated that in his view these distinctions between different categories of judge were out of date and should be abolished. He proposed that every judge should have immunity "when he is acting judicially." The other members of the court limited their decision to the immunity of the class of judge in question so that doubt remains.

The immunity given to judges is also extended to the lawyers, the jury, the parties and witnesses in respect of anything said in the course of a trial. It is felt that this freedom will lead to the easier discovery of the truth and will also stop further civil actions being brought, thus possibly preventing endless litigation. Even the press has the benefit of immunity, in that newspaper and broadcast reports of judicial proceedings, provided they are fair and accurate and contemporaneous, are absolutely privileged from an action for defamation.

6. Contempt of Court

Judges have considerable powers to control persons appearing before them in litigation. They can punish individuals who are in contempt of the court; this misconduct can take a number of forms:

(i) contempt on the face of the court, *e.g.* throwing eggs at the judge; or attempting to introduce "laughing gas" into court: *Balogh* v. *St. Albans Crown Court* (1975);

(ii) contempt by disobeying a court order, *e.g.* continuing to publish a libel after the court orders a person to desist;

(iii) contempt by prejudicing a pending trial, *e.g.* publishing information about a person about to be tried which might influence possible jurymen: *R.* v. *Bolam, ex parte Haigh* (1949) where the editor of the *Daily Mirror* was sent to prison for three months and the paper was heavily fined for a blatant instance of the publication of an article prejudicing a pending murder trial.

A person sentenced for contempt of court by a High Court judge can appeal to the Court of Appeal. The law on the subject is largely to be found in the Contempt of Court Act 1981.

7. The Judicial Function

All judges and magistrates on appointment take the judicial oath under the Promissory Oaths Act 1868, "to do right to all manner of people after the laws and usages of this realm without fear or favour, affection or ill-will."

Judges receive no overt training in preparation for their change of role and this has been the subject of comment. A brilliant advocate may after all make an unsatisfactory judge. A recent innovation is a Judicial Studies Board which, it is hoped, will assist judges in their exacting role by organising lectures and residential seminars and by providing helpful literature. It currently publishes a Bulletin which is mainly concerned with sentencing policy in the Crown Court.

The function of the judge is to preside at trials of civil, and possibly criminal, cases, to conduct the hearing according to the accepted rules of procedure and evidence, to give rulings on points of law and, where appropriate, to sum up the factual evidence in order to assist the jury. If there is no jury the judge himself hears and determines the case by giving a reasoned explanation of the legal principles which he has decided to apply.

In giving judgment the judge is inevitably creating new law— judge-made law. The decision must be consistent with existing legal principles, and as such must be linked to a consideration of previous case decisions by earlier judges. This system is known as the doctrine of judicial precedent and will be considered at length in Chapter 11. Even where the judge's task is to interpret a word or phrase appearing in a statute, he will still need to be guided by other previous judicial interpretations relevant to the one with which he is concerned. There are two ways of looking at the role of the judge in giving judgment—one is to see his function as *"jus dicere,"* simply saying what the law is, and always has been, on the facts of the particular case; the other is to regard it as *"jus dare,"* meaning to give or create the law applicable to the facts revealed. On either view the discretion of the judge is very limited in view of the application of the doctrine of judicial precedent.

8. Criticism

Criticism of the judiciary usually takes the form that the social and educational background of the persons appointed to be judges is so similar that the judiciary is inevitably out of sympathy with modern social tendencies, and has long failed to have any understanding of the working conditions, attitudes of mind and aspirations of the mass of the population. It is certainly true that most of the High Court and Appeal Court judges received a public school education followed by legal studies at Oxbridge and then call to the Bar.

Another criticism attaches to the appointment of judges. Pressure appears to be increasing for appointments to be recommended by a Board or Commission of legal specialists rather than to continue to be at the sole discretion of the Lord Chancellor or Prime Minister.

In order to justify the existing arrangement the Lord Chancellor's Department in 1986 published a booklet entitled "Judicial Appointments."

9. Judicial Offices

Lord Chancellor. The senior appointment in the judicial system of England and Wales is the Lord Chancellor, or, as his formal title has it, the Lord High Chancellor. Paradoxically, in view of the emphasis which is placed on the independence of the judiciary, the person appointed receives the honour for political reasons, being invited to accept the office by the Prime Minister in the same way as any other member of the administration is selected. The Lord Chancellor, consequently, is a prominent member of the Government and invariably has a seat in the Cabinet. He will have achieved considerable eminence in his dual legal and political roles before attaining the office, and once appointed his duties cause him to be the complete denial of the constitutional doctrine of the separation of powers. As well as heading a department of the executive with substantial responsibilities—the Lord Chancellor's office consists of over 10,000 staff—he is also the apparent chairman of the House of Lords sitting there on the Woolsack in full ceremonial dress. In the judicial sphere, although his other duties preclude his acting as a judge regularly, he is the senior judge of both the House of Lords and the Court of Appeal, and also for historical reasons the Chancery Division of the High Court of Justice. Nonetheless, his tenure of office depends upon the Prime Minister. He can be replaced at any time and, if the Government resigns, the Lord Chancellor like all government Ministers goes out of office forthwith. His present salary is £77,000.

Lord Chief Justice. The Lord Chief Justice is the senior judge of the Queen's Bench Division of the High Court of Justice. He can take part in the ordinary work of the division but more often he is engaged in presiding over the Court of Appeal (Criminal Division) or the Queen's Bench Divisional Court. He is made a peer of the realm on appointment but he does not normally sit in House of Lords cases. His salary is £77,400 per annum.

Master of the Rolls. The Master of the Rolls is the title of the judge who organises the work of and presides over the Court of Appeal (Civil Division). He is responsible for the Public Record Office as his title indicates. He also formally admits newly qualified solicitors to the roll of the court so enabling them to practise. His salary is £71,400 per annum.

The President of the Family Division of the High Court of Justice. The President of the Family Division of the High Court is the senior judge in that division. He organises the work of the division, taking part in it himself, and also sitting to hear appeals in the Family Divisional Court. His salary is £68,400 per annum.

The office of Vice-Chancellor. The Vice-Chancellor, under the Lord Chancellor, is the senior judge of the Chancery Division. He is responsible for the organisation and management of the business of the Division. His salary is £68,400.

The Lords of Appeal in Ordinary. There can now be 11 Lords of Appeal in Ordinary. They are appointed under section 6 of the Appellate Jurisdiction Act 1876 and form, as the House of Lords in its judicial capacity, the final appeal court for all cases heard in England, Wales, Scotland and Northern Ireland, except Scottish criminal cases. More often called "the Law Lords," they are made peers on appointment, but by convention they take only a limited part in the legislative work of the House of Lords and they do not engage in political controversy. At least one of the Law Lords will be from Scotland and one will be from Northern Ireland. The hearing of cases takes place in a committee room of the Houses of Parliament at Westminster. The basic qualification for appointment is 15 years' experience as a barrister or two years in high judicial office. Virtually all English appointments follow experience in the Court of Appeal. The annual salary is £71,400.

Lords Justices of Appeal. The judges who sit in the Court of Appeal are called Lords Justices of Appeal. There are now 22 Lords Justices of Appeal and appointments to this office are made from High Court judges. As they are already knighted, on appointment they are made privy counsellors. Fifteen years' experience as a barrister is an essential prerequisite to appointment unless the person concerned is already a High Court judge and has had two years' experience in office. Appeal cases which they try are heard at the Royal Courts of Justice in the Strand. The annual salary is £68,400.

High Court judges. The maximum number of High Court judges is now 80. New judges are allocated to one of the three Divisions of the High Court but theoretically such a judge can be asked to serve in any Division. At present there are 49 in the Queen's Bench Division, 12 in the Chancery Division and 16 in the Family Division. High Court judges are selected either from circuit judges or from the practising Bar, and are knighted on appointment. They must be barristers of 10 years' standing. High Court judges are addressed as "Your Lordship" and are known as puisne judges. They operate from the Royal Courts of Justice in the Strand where cases are heard, but certain Queen's Bench Division judges have special responsibility for the work of the Crown Court in the centres designated under the Courts Act 1971. The annual salary is £62,100.

Circuit judges. The Courts Act 1971 divided England and Wales into six regions and made arrangements for each region to be staffed by High Court judges, circuit judges and recorders. The former county court judges became circuit judges and some 373 full time appointments have been made. A circuit judge must have had 10 years' experience as a barrister or have been a recorder for three years. He is addressed as "Your Honour" and the salary is £41,500 per annum. Circuit judges as well as their Crown Court responsibilities can also preside in county courts; they thus have a mixed civil and criminal role.

Recorders. Part time appointments as recorders were also instituted for barristers and solicitors of 10 years' standing to assist in the Crown Court. The main obligation is to serve as a judge for not less than 20 days in the year. Some 432 appointments have been made including approximately 50 solicitors. It will be noted that a solicitor, who serves as a recorder for three years, is eligible for appointment as a circuit judge. Recorders are addressed as "Sir."

Magistrates. For the hearing of certain criminal and some civil cases, local citizens have for many centuries been appointed. They are not legally qualified and in that sense they are not properly entitled to be called judges; on the other hand this vast group of laymen, estimated to be some 26,000 strong does, nonetheless, hear and determine the vast majority of criminal offences in England and Wales. The figure is said to be 97 per cent.

In London and in some of the larger cities it has been found necessary to have qualified lawyers acting full-time on a salaried basis as magistrates. These are known as metropolitan stipendiary magistrates in London, and as stipendiary magistrates elsewhere. In total there are 55.

A magistrate is addressed as "Your Worship" and is entitled to use the initials J.P. for "Justice of the Peace," this being the original name for a magistrate.

A full account of the part played in the legal system by magistrates is given in Chapter 3.

Chairmen of Tribunals. In Chapter 9 the importance of tribunals in the English legal system is examined. In most tribunals the Chairman will be a lawyer presiding either full-time or part-time. Some full-time appointments, for example, as Social Security Commissioners or in Industrial Tribunals, are akin to being the judge of a minor court.

Holders of other important legal offices. The Attorney-General is, like the Lord Chancellor, a political appointment, chosen by the Prime Minister from government members of the House of Commons. Normally the person selected is a Queen's Counsel who has been elected an M.P. and his main task is to act as legal adviser to the government departments. He also appears for the Crown in important legal cases. He is regarded as the head of the English Bar and is paid a salary of approximately £34,000 per annum. His deputy is the Solicitor-General, also a government member of the House of Commons and an eminent barrister. His salary is approximately £28,000 per annum. Legal fees which they earn are set off against their salaries. They are called the Law Officers.

The Director of Public Prosecutions was originally appointed in 1879 to ensure that legal cases of major importance are dealt with consistently and effectively, and that advice about criminal law matters should be available to chief constables. The Director must be a barrister or solicitor of 10 years' standing but he is not a politician. He has a staff of lawyers to assist him and he can employ counsel and solicitors to handle cases on his behalf. Under the Prosecution of Offences Act 1985 the Director of Public Prosecutions heads the national Crown Prosecution Service. The Attorney General answers in Parliament for the work of the Director's office.

Terminology. When law reports refer to the judge giving judgment in a case, a system of abbreviations is used. These a student will need to recognise. Although current holders of offices are shown this is by way of example.

Lord Chancellor	Lord Hailsham L.C.
Lord Chief Justice	Lord Lane C.J.
Master of the Rolls	Sir John Donaldson M.R.
President of the Family Division	Arnold P.
Vice-Chancellor	Browne-Wilkinson V.C.
Lords of Appeal in Ordinary	Lord Bridge
Lords Justices of Appeal	Woolf L.J.
High Court judges	Webster J.

3. Magistrates

1. The Lay Principle

The preceding chapters have been mainly concerned with the part played by the professional in the administration of justice, from the initial difficulty of obtaining entry to the legal profession as a practising barrister or solicitor, to the invitation ultimately extended to the experienced barrister to become a judge. In this and the next chapter attention is directed to the contribution made by the layman to the English legal system; first, in the form of the lay magistrate, making a major contribution to the work of the courts, and then as a juryman, taking the responsibility for decisions of fact at the most serious criminal, and some important civil, trials.

The combination of professional and layman in the system is generally felt to be an excellent arrangement, since it ensures that the law, and in particular criminal law, is kept in close contact with representatives of the public who are affected by it. It is argued that this helps to preserve a respect for law throughout the community. As there are estimated to be some 26,000 lay magistrates at the present time, their share in the administration of justice is undeniably of first-rank importance.

2. Appointment

Magistrates or, as the older title has it, Justices of the Peace, are appointed by the Crown on the advice of the Lord Chancellor (or the Chancellor of the Duchy of Lancaster for that area). Each area which has a separate body of justices has a commission from the Crown, and the names of new justices are added to the Schedule attached to the commission. The magistrate so appointed can carry out his functions only within the area covered by the commission, and it is a requirement that the magistrate must continue to live within 15 miles of that area. If he moves his place of residence more than this distance , then his name is removed from the commission and is placed on the supplemental list, but he may, in due course, be allowed to sit as a magistrate again in the area to which he has moved. Before he can do so his name will have to be added, on the Lord Chancellor's authority, to that commission.

Inevitably the Lord Chancellor in recommending names for appointment has to seek local guidance. This he does by having 190 advisory committees covering England and Wales. The composition of the committees is not generally known although the tendency in recent years has been to publish the name of the secretary, so that local organisations and members of the public can put forward the names of individuals whom they consider to be worthy of appointment. In the occasional instance the Lord Chancellor has authorised the insertion of a local newspaper advertisement inviting nominations.

The great difficulty in obtaining a suitable balance in the composition of the local magistracy is that there is a natural tendency for candidates to be chosen from individuals prominent in local public life. Consequently, over the years the majority of appointments have been made from members of the local party political organisations, with the inevitable criticism following that this is akin to a "spoils" system. It is a difficult problem and one which is never likely to be resolved to every one's satisfaction.

The persons, who are selected, are chosen as responsible and respected members of their local community, capable of deciding cases without bias and possessed of sound commonsense. Until 1906 justices had to have a property qualification and women only became eligible for appointment in 1919. Although members of the legal profession can be appointed, and all judges are *ex officio* justices of the peace, there is no requirement that persons appointed must have had legal training.

In the early history of the office, remuneration for the service given was a feature of the appointment, but this has long since ceased to be the case. Magistrates receive no remuneration. They are however entitled to travelling expenses and to certain subsistence payments, if their residence is more than three miles from the court house. Another provision enables a magistrate to claim reimbursement for loss of earnings or other necessary expenditure incurred as a result of attending court. The scale of reimbursement is approved by Parliament.

3. Training

Because magistrates are not legally trained there used to be considerable criticism that people were taking part in the administration of justice without knowing anything about legal principles or court procedure. Present practice requires every magistrate on appointment to undergo a training course arranged on a local part-time basis. Additional training courses are arranged for magistrates wishing to participate in juvenile court and domestic court work. Over all supervision now rests with the Judicial Studies Board.

4. Removal

Dismissal

The Lord Chancellor retains a discretion to remove the name of any magistrate from the commission for any reason he thinks fit. On the rare occasion when this drastic step is taken, it will usually be because the magistrate has either been guilty of some serious personal misconduct or because he has failed to carry out his duties as a magistrate in some important respect. The magistrate who announces that he will not enforce an Act of Parliament because he disagrees with its provisions is certain to find that his name will be promptly removed from the commission.

Retirement

Magistrates retire at the age of 70 when their names are placed on a supplemental list. This means that the magistrate may no longer sit on the bench but he can still deal with certain paper work and so retain the status of a justice of the peace.

5. Organisation

Every county has a separate commission of the peace, as have the London commission areas and the City of London. Magistrates consequently are appointed on a local basis and they may only sit therefore to try cases within their locality. In total there are now approximately 700 magistrates' courts.

Each commission area will have its own magistrates' courts committee and this is the representative body which speaks for the individual magistrate as well as attending to more mundane matters like the provision of court rooms and supervising the rota of magistrates to attend the Crown Court.

Nationally the Magistrates' Association speaks for the magistrates as a collective body. It publishes a magazine called appropriately "The Magistrate."

6. "The Bench"

For the hearing of a case in the magistrates' court a minimum of two and a maximum of seven magistrates take part. It is not usual for more than five to sit. Collectively they are known as "the Bench" and they are addressed as "Your Worships." An annual election of a chairman of the bench is held, the choice being made by the justices by a secret ballot. When the magistrates sit as a juvenile court, that is trying cases which involve persons under the age of 17, statutory provisions govern the position. It is usual for three magistrates to sit, all of whom are drawn from a special panel and one, at least, must be a woman. The same is true when the court sits to deal with domestic proceedings.

7. Clerk to the Justices

Because of the lay nature of the magistrates it has been customary for many years for every bench of magistrates to have a legally qualified clerk as adviser. The clerk's part in the proceedings is to administer the court and to give legal advice to the bench where this is necessary. In practice the clerk and the magistrates have to work out the relationship, because the clerk must not take over the duties of the magistrates. To this end he must not go with them when they retire to arrive at their decision in a case, nor must he be allowed to dominate the proceedings.

Originally many clerks to the justices were local solicitors in private practice holding the appointment in a part-time capacity. Present policy is to have full-time clerks, barristers or solicitors of not less than five years' standing, with, if geographically necessary, one clerk covering a number of courts. At a recent count there were 333 clerks in England and Wales, 309 full-time and 24 part-time.

8. Stipendiary Magistrates

The pressure of business in the great cities has meant that as well as having lay magistrates it has been thought desirable to employ full-time salaried lawyers to assist with the work of magistrates. These are called stipendiary magistrates, and in London, metropolitan stipendiary magistrates. Stipendiary magistrates can be appointed by county or district councils on the recommendation of the Lord Chancellor from barristers or solicitors of seven years' standing; metropolitan stipendiary magistrates are directly appointed by the Lord Chancellor and must be barristers or solicitors of 10 years' standing.

There are at present 55 stipendiary magistrates in England and Wales so that the power to appoint stipendiaries is not widely used. Two factors which are relevant to this are, first, that the lay magistrates prefer the existing system and, second, that being a stipendiary magistrate is not very rewarding in terms of work. It would be difficult not to become bored with day-to-day court work at this level. Public opinion does not seem to have a strong preference one way or the other, and at least the lay magistrate does not have to be paid!

9. History

The justice of the peace has a very long history as an institution in the legal system. It has been claimed that a royal proclamation in 1195, which set up knights of the peace to assist the sheriff in the maintenance of law and order, was the origin of the justice of the peace. Clearer evidence comes from statutes in 1327 and 1361 under which "good and lawful men" were to be "assigned to keep the peace," holding administrative rather than judicial authority, and like the present-day justice not legally qualified and acting part-time. The title justice of the peace is first used in the 1361 statute. In 1363 a statute required four quarter sessions to be held annually, and gradually the power to deal with criminal cases was added to the administrative work. From 1496 justices were permitted to try the minor—summary—criminal cases locally at petty sessions, instead of at quarter sessions, so giving rise to the major jurisdiction of magistrates in their courts of summary jurisdiction at the present time. The administrative responsibility of magistrates for many local government functions remained with them until the setting up of the modern elected authorities under the Local Government Acts of 1888 and 1894. Traces of it are still to be seen in the statutory one-third membership of magistrates on police committees, and in their membership of the Crown Court.

10. Functions of Magistrates

Magistrates have an important role in the hearing of both criminal and civil cases. This section considers the part played by magistrates in the courts but leaves to Chapter 7 the procedure which operates in those courts.

Criminal

Criminal offences fall into two categories; they are broadly either summary or indictable. The less serious are the summary offences and these are the offences which Parliament has decreed that magistrates shall determine. They extend from such criminal conduct as drunkenness in a public place to minor theft, and from many road traffic offences to minor assault. Such cases are heard and determined by a bench of from two to seven magistrates in what is formally known as a court of summary jurisdiction. It will be seen that these criminal cases are basically concerned with matters of fact, rather than law, and it is thus not as unsatisfactory as it might seem to allow persons lacking legal qualifications to try such cases.

In many instances the statute defining the summary offence will set out the maximum punishment which can be awarded. A magistrate sitting alone can award at the most a £1 fine or 14 days' imprisonment. In general two or more magistrates' sentencing powers are limited to six months' imprisonment and/or a £2,000 fine. If the same person is convicted of two or more offences at the one hearing the power to imprison is increased to 12 months. If the magistrates decide that their powers are not adequate for an appropriate sentence in a particular case, they can send the person concerned to the Crown Court for sentence since that court has much greater sentencing powers.

The number of summary cases heard annually by magistrates is approximately two million, which is 95 per cent. of all criminal cases tried in England and Wales. From time to time proposals are made seeking to increase the number of cases triable by magistrates by transferring into the summary category certain offences, such as certain assault, theft and damage to property offences where at present the accused may choose to be tried by a jury.

In indictable cases, which are the more serious criminal offences, covering such matters as rape, burglary and homicide, magistrates do not have the power to try the case themselves. The trial must be by judge and jury. However, before the case comes to trial, there is a preliminary inquiry stage where, usually, two magistrates sit to examine the prosecution case. The purpose of this preliminary inquiry is to ensure that the prosecution acts promptly in preparing its case, and that the evidence available through prosecution witnesses reveals a prima facie case against the person accused and warrants his being put on trial. If they are satisfied, the magistrates commit the accused for trial by jury to the Crown Court. Consequently, this procedure is known as "committal proceedings."

Until the Criminal Justice Act 1967 the procedure followed at this stage involved the prosecution in presenting its case in full by the calling of all the prosecution witnesses and the copying out in longhand by the clerk to the justices of all the evidence which they gave. Each witness then swore on oath to the truth of what he had said and signed the "deposition" accordingly. The Magistrates Courts Act 1980 now provides that if both prosecution and defence legal representatives agree, written statements of evidence can be presented to the magistrates and they can commit for trial on the strength of these documents. This is often known as new style committal in contrast to the old style full scale proceedings. It will be noted that the defence chooses the form of the committal proceedings, old style or new style. In general this has substantially cut down the time formerly spent on the preliminary inquiry.

The Crown Court

The Courts Act 1971 which abolished Assizes and Quarter Sessions put in their place the Crown Court. Magistrates have a significant part to play in the operation of the Crown Court since they are called upon to sit, as judges, with the circuit judge or the recorder in the hearing of certain cases. For example, in the hearing of an appeal from the decision of a magistrates' court in a summary case, or where magistrates have committed a defendant for sentence to the Crown Court, not less than two nor more than four magistrates must sit with the judge. At an indictable trial a regular judge of the Crown Court may sit with not more than four magistrates. The magistrates must accept the judge's ruling on points of law but otherwise the decision of the court is by a majority. If necessary the presiding judge has a casting vote.

Civil

Although magistrates are usually regarded as playing a vital part in the criminal court structure, they have also been given a substantial jurisdiction by Parliament over a number of civil matters.

Some of these matters remain with the magistrates as a result of their history. The responsibility which the justices of the peace had from the time of Elizabeth I in administering the poor law in the locality led to their having a special concern for the maintenance of the illegitimate child. One result has been that applications for what are now known as affiliation orders are still made to the local magistrates. Under such an order a maintenance payment of a weekly sum can be required of the putative father, continuing until the child reaches the age of 16.

From legislation in the later years of the nineteenth century, magistrates derived a responsibility of much larger significance in the making of separation and maintenance orders in matrimonial disputes. The Court has to see that a man maintains his wife and children, and this can be done by making an attachment of earnings order where this is considered appropriate. In reaching a decision the magistrates are concerned to hear evidence relating to alleged desertion, persistent cruelty, adultery or wilful neglect to maintain. Because of the highly personal nature of the evidence the public is excluded and three magistrates, including at least one woman, sit to hear the case.

Other matters of a family law nature also fall to be decided by magistrates. These include applications concerning the custody, upbringing and maintenance of children, adoption proceedings and children in need of care and protection. This jurisdiction could well be affected if the proposed Family Court ever became a reality.

Magistrates have also long been responsible under licensing law for determining all the many and various applications which are required to be made under that legislation.

4. The Jury

1. "The Bulwark of our Liberties"

The introduction of laymen as the arbiters on matters of fact in judicial hearings is of long standing in the English legal system. Criticism has been directed at the use of juries. It is argued that the 12 laymen are easily swayed by the eloquence of a barrister against the weight of the evidence, and that the average intelligence of such a group of citizens, called to attend against their wishes, is in contrast to the complexity of many of the cases in which they have to give a verdict. Against this view are many judicial pronouncements in praise of the jury, one of the more striking being Lord Devlin's view that "the jury is the lamp which shows that freedom lives," and another is Lord Denning's statement that it is "the bulwark of our liberties."

The Roskill report on Fraud (1986) has renewed the debate by calling for the use of "assessors" instead of juries in certain complicated fraud cases. It is also being suggested that more offences should be designated summary offences, so that trial by jury would be available only for the most serious criminal cases.

2. Selection of Jurors

The Juries Act 1974 specifies that every person between the ages of 18 and 65, who is registered on the annual electoral register as an elector and who has lived in this country for at least five years since the age of 13, is qualified to serve as a juror. The Act goes on to detail certain disqualifications and exemptions. For example members of the legal profession and clergymen are ineligible, whilst persons convicted of criminal offences, and who are serving or have served in the last ten years sentences of imprisonment, detention or youth custody of three months or more or have been to Borstal are disqualified. A suspended sentence of imprisonment or detention or

33

the making of a community service order, all within the ten-year period, act as a disqualification. So does being placed on probation within a five-year period. A person who has been sentenced to imprisonment or youth custody for five years or more is permanently disqualified. Certain members of the community, such as members of the armed forces and doctors, may be excused from jury service if they so wish, whilst the court has a discretion to release a person called for jury service if proper cause is shown.

Proposed legislation, if enacted, will permit persons aged 65 to 70 to sit as jurors if they so wish. It will also remove the right of the defence to challenge jurors on a peremptory basis. This emphasises that a jury is intended to be a cross-section of the community.

3. Rights of Jurors

Modern society recognises that the individuals called to serve on a jury must not be allowed to suffer financially as a result of such public service. The legislation permits a juror to receive reimbursement of his travelling expenses, a subsistence allowance and, where appropriate, a financial loss allowance. This is intended to compensate the juror who has had, for example, to employ additional labour in his business because he has had to serve on the jury and has thus suffered a direct loss of earnings.

The obligation to serve on the jury is compulsory, and personal inconvenience, such as having to cancel a holiday, is no excuse. Medical evidence, or compelling business reasons, are possible methods of escape. The complexity of modern crime, which can lead to cases continuing over a number of weeks, is another factor which causes the call to jury service to be something generally disliked. If a person declines to serve on a jury, the judge may order him to be present in court throughout the trial of that case.

An interesting historical survival is the rule that jurors cannot be punished if they bring in a perverse verdict contrary to the direction of the judge. This was laid down in *Bushell's Case* in 1670 where two Quakers were charged with tumultuous assembly. The jury were ordered to convict, but instead returned a verdict of "not guilty." The judge sent the jury to prison until they should pay a fine by way of punishment. On appeal it was held that the fine and imprisonment could not be allowed to stand. The Ponting trial of 1985 saw a jury bring in a verdict of "not guilty" in an Official Secrets Act case where a conviction had been expected.

4. Function of the Jury

The purpose of having the jury is to enable the vital decision on fact in a case to be taken by a small cross-section of the community, rather than for it to be left entirely in the hands of the lawyers. Thus, in criminal cases tried on indictment at the Crown Court, the guilt of the person accused has to be established to the satisfaction of the 12 jurors in the case beyond all reasonable doubt (but a majority verdict may be permissible, see p. 36, below). At the conclusion of the case it is for the jury, after hearing the judge's "summing up" of the prosecution and defence case, to retire and consider their verdict in private. On the pronouncement of that verdict by the foreman of the jury the accused is found either "guilty" or "not guilty." If "not guilty" he is said to be acquitted and is free to leave the court; if "guilty" the accused becomes "the prisoner," and the sentence of the court is the responsibility of the judge. He will first hear the criminal record of the prisoner and then a plea in mitigation of sentence, which is made by defence counsel. The jury has no part to play in the decision as to sentence. Equally the jury has no part in decisions which are concerned with law or legal procedure. Since the 12 laymen involved are likely to be devoid of any knowledge of law, this is not without reason. In practice the judge at a trial will, on occasions, have to ask the jury to retire, so that he can decide on a point of law which has arisen and which will be argued by the counsel in the case. In criminal cases this is most often about the admissibility of evidence, in the form of statements or confessions alleged to have been made by the accused on his arrest.

As will be seen in Chapter 7 criminal offences are for trial purposes designated as (1) triable on indictment only, (2) triable summarily only, and (3) triable either way. This latter category is governed by the procedure laid down in the legislation and so jury trial in criminal cases is available to those charged with an offence triable on indictment only and to those who so qualify under the triable either way provisions.

In civil cases the jury is used less and less. Although under court rules a jury of eight may be called in the county court at the discretion of the judge, in practice the use of such a jury is not common. In the High Court too the tendency is for cases to be heard by the judge alone; by the High Court, the Queen's Bench Division is intended, because juries are never used in the Chancery Division and only very rarely in the Family Division. In the following types of case there is, by section 69 of the Supreme Court Act 1981, a right to jury trial: libel, slander, malicious prosecution, false imprisonment and fraud. Even here jury trial can be refused if a prolonged examination of documents, or accounts, or a scientific or local investigation, or other complex material is involved. In all other cases the judge has a discretion to allow a jury trial, but he must exercise this discretion judicially. The trend away from jury trial in civil cases has been comparatively rapid, since as recently as 1933 50 per cent. of cases involved a jury. Following the legislation of that year the figure fell steadily, and in the years before 1966 was estimated to be as low as 2 per cent. Then in *Ward* v. *James* (1966) a five-judge Court of Appeal decided that trial by judge alone should be the usual mode of trial, save where statute provided otherwise, or where a judge decided that the exceptional circumstances warranted it. This decline in the use of the jury in the High Court can be accounted for on two grounds: one is the inconsistency in the award of damages, and the other is the exorbitant figures for damages which sometimes resulted. It is obviously easier to achieve consistency in the scale of damages for personal injuries if that matter is left to the judges, and this is the course now favoured.

The jury is not used in civil or criminal appeal courts because there the case almost always turns on points of law; nor is it used in the magistrates' courts where presumably it is felt that the magistrates provide the lay element and the importance of summary cases does not warrant imposing on the time of 12 members of the community.

The coroner, whose task it is to inquire into the cause of death whenever a person dies other than from natural causes, can, and in some circumstances must, call a jury for the inquest. The coroner's jury can number from seven to 11 and it will, after hearing the evidence, return a verdict as to the cause of death and the coroner must record this verdict. The general intention is to ensure that deaths are thoroughly investigated, and, where the death is the result of an accident, to try and prevent a recurrence.

5. Majority Verdicts

For centuries the fundamental requirement in the English legal system was that the verdict of the jury in both civil and criminal trials should be unanimous. If unanimity could not be achieved then a re-trial was necessary.

In the 1960s there was increasing criticism of this requirement, particularly on the part of the police who pointed out that one member of the jury if "got at" by the criminal fraternity could cause a re-trial by simply refusing to agree with the other 11 jurors in a criminal case. After much debate the Criminal Justice Act 1967 made provision for a majority verdict to be accepted by the judge in a criminal case at his discretion provided that not more than two members of the jury were in the minority (or one member if the jury is reduced to 11 or 10 in number) and provided also that the jury had spent at least two hours seeking to achieve unanimity. If the verdict was "guilty" the fact that it was a majority verdict had to be disclosed in open court.

The majority verdict provisions were extended to civil cases, where a jury had been called, by the Courts Act 1971.

All the provisions concerning majority verdicts have now been consolidated in the Juries Act 1974.

6. History

The jury as an English legal institution can claim a very long history in the course of which it has completely changed its role. At present the essential element of the jury system is the fact that the 12 persons called for jury service are completely unknown to the person accused, and thus can give him a fair trial free of any bias. Every effort is made to ensure that the jury have no prior knowledge of the case, and will be able to reach their verdict entirely on the evidence presented at the trial. Originally, in the earliest days of the English legal system, the jury's role was a combination of local police and prosecutor. Centuries before a paid police force came into being, the responsibility for law and order was a community responsibility. This led to the local "jury" for the hundred having to arrest suspected offenders, and then bring these offenders before the itinerant judge when he visited the locality and lay the facts of the case before him. There was nothing unusual in this use of local representatives in the early community. It can be seen also in the local inquiries which led to the creation of Domesday Book, and the system of inquisitions post mortem—the inquiry held on a death as to the ownership of the lands and goods of the deceased—where again considerable reliance seems to have been placed on local representatives. Throughout the Middle Ages the local community voice is frequently sought in the settlement of litigation disputes concerning the ownership and tenancy of land and the right to an advowson (the right to present to the living of a church).

It was only very gradually and with the passage of centuries that the use of the jury in its modern role, as the judges of fact, developed. Even then the original concept continued to exist and this led to the existence of a grand jury and a petty jury. The grand jury numbering 24 members met only at the start of assizes or quarter sessions in order to find a true bill of indictment against the accused. Since the accused had previously undergone the preliminary inquiry by magistrates, who had heard the prosecution case and had decided to commit the accused for trial, the decision of the grand jury became a complete formality. Nonetheless it reveals clearly the original role of the jury as the presenter of the accused for trial. The grand jury was substantially abolished by the Administration of Justice (Miscellaneous Provisions) Act 1933 and finally brought to an end by the Criminal Justice Act 1948. The petty jury of 12 members on the other hand came into being in the thirteenth century to take the place of trial by ordeal, which the ecclesiastical authorities then saw fit to condemn. It became increasingly distinct in its function from the grand jury, although it long maintained its approach of the jury being local witnesses of fact deciding matters from their local knowledge. It was the fifteenth century before the petty jury assumed its modern role in criminal trials as judges of fact.

In civil cases the jury appears to have had its origin in the Assizes of Clarendon in 1166, and the Assizes of Northampton in 1176, establishing the grand and petty assizes. Here again the jury was at first called to decide a case from its local knowledge, and only with the passage of time did it become an impartial judge of the facts. The system allowed for trial to be in two parts—the local jury would hear and deal with the case locally, and then send their findings to the judges at Westminster where the judgment would be given. Jury trial was for centuries as widely used in civil as in criminal cases, and it is only the last 100 years since the Common Law Procedure Act 1854 which has seen the substantial falling off in the use of the jury in civil cases.

The petty jury nonetheless remains a vital element in the English legal system and, as has been seen, it continues to play a major part in the administration of justice at the present time.

5. Civil Courts

1. The Civil Court Structure

In all legal systems a distinction is drawn between civil law and criminal law, and generally a separate system of courts and of court procedure accompanies this division. The English legal system follows this pattern; and so this chapter will describe the civil court structure whilst Chapter 6 will examine the criminal court structure and Chapter 7 will outline the procedure followed in the civil and criminal courts.

The fundamental difference between civil law and criminal law is that in criminal law the state is concerned to enforce law and order in the community by ensuring that an accepted code of conduct is everywhere observed. In civil law the state plays little part, other than to provide the forum for the settlement of disputes between individuals. These include breach of contract cases, disputes about liability for alleged civil misconduct—torts—and property disagreements, *e.g.* as between a landlord and a tenant, all of which are civil law matters. The distinction between civil law and criminal law will be developed in greater detail in Chapter 12 where the classification of English law is considered.

2. The County Court

Since 1846 the county court has provided a nation-wide system for the trial of civil cases where a comparatively small amount of money is involved.

There are some 300 districts in England and Wales in which a county court is held at least once a month, and these towns and cities are divided up into some 60 circuits. Each circuit has its own judge and in the larger cities there may be more than one judge attached to the circuit. As a result of the Courts Act 1971 the judge will be a circuit judge who may also sit in the Crown Court for that area. As well as a judge, each circuit has to have a registrar, a solicitor of seven years' standing, and he will be assisted in the general administration of the work of the court by a clerical staff of civil servants. Among his tasks are dealing with interlocutory matters (matters arising during a trial such as an application for discovery of documents) holding the pre-trial review, considering applications for adjournment, taxing costs, and also disposing of undefended cases or claims involving small amounts. This latter role in 1985 saw the registrar, acting as an arbitrator, make awards in something over 44,000 small claims. The administration of the system vests in the Lord Chancellor, who has power to alter the arrangements as circumstances change. The organisation of the county court system does not follow county boundaries and so to that extent the term "county" court is a misnomer.

For the hearing of a case the judge sits alone. In theory a jury of eight can be called, but in practice this is very rare. For claims where less than £500 is involved the registrar can act as judge. An appeal from the registrar's finding goes to the judge, whilst an appeal from the judge goes, subject to certain conditions, to the Court of Appeal (Civil Division). These conditions are, that leave is necessary for appeal where the amount at issue does not exceed one half of the relevant county court limit. Exceptions to this rule include applications for an injunction and actions involving custody and access to children.

The actual jurisdiction of the county court can be listed as:

(i) actions founded on contract and in tort not exceeding £5,000 (but not libel or slander);

(ii) actions concerning land of a rateable value not exceeding £1,000 per annum;

(iii) equity matters concerning, for example, trusts, mortgages or partnerships, under £30,000 in value;

(iv) probate disputes where the deceased person's estate is valued at less than £30,000;

(v) company winding up where the paid-up capital of the company is less than £10,000;

(vi) miscellaneous functions connected with adoption, guardianship of minors and legitimacy;

(vii) (some courts) admiralty matters, *i.e.* shipping cases where the claim does not exceed £5,000; or in salvage cases not exceeding £15,000;

(viii) (some courts) bankruptcy matters with unlimited jurisdiction (not London);

(ix) (some courts) divorce petitions, if undefended, together with consequent maintenance and custody claims;

(x) (some courts) cases brought by the Race Relations Board alleging discrimination under the Race Relations legislation;

(xi) jurisdiction derived from some 150 statutes dealing with a wide variety of subject-matter.

This list is not exhaustive and so for a full grasp of the law as it applies in the county court, reference must be made to the County Courts Act 1984 as amended, and to the County Court Rules 1981 as amended. For practitioners the annual *County Court Practice*—the Green Book as it is known—is essential.

Every effort is made to persuade a claimant to bring his action in the county court, if the amount involved is within the county court limits. If the case is brought in the High Court when it could have been brought in the county court, in most circumstances the successful party will only be allowed his costs on the county court scale. This may mean that the successful party is out of pocket, since the difference between the two court scales is considerable. It is also possible for the parties to agree to have their case heard in the county court even when the claim is for more than £5,000. It is also open to the High Court to remit cases for trial to the county court where it thinks this course desirable.

The number of cases begun in the county courts in 1985 was 2,162,229. This represents some 80 per cent. of the total of civil proceedings begun in all the civil courts and explains why this court is sometimes called "the most important court in the land." The figures are, however, misleading in that the vast majority of county court cases are settled, withdrawn or abandoned without a trial. In 1985 approximately 10 per cent. of cases begun were actually tried before the registrar or the judge.

3. The High Court of Justice

The High Court of Justice and the Court of Appeal were brought into being as the Supreme Court of Judicature under the Judicature Acts 1873–1875. At that time the High Court consisted of five Divisions—the Queen's Bench, Chancery, Probate, Divorce and Admiralty, Exchequer and Common Pleas. The last two Divisions were merged in the Queen's Bench Division in 1880 and the remaining three Divisions continued unaltered from then until the Administration of Justice Act 1970 redistributed the functions of the Probate, Divorce and Admiralty Division and gave it the new title of the Family Division.

There is a maximum number of 80 High Court judges appointed to the three Divisions according to the pressure of work. When appointed the judge has to be prepared to serve in any of the Divisions, but in practice judges tend as a general rule to continue to serve in the Division to which they have been allocated. At present there are 49 judges in the Queen's Bench Division, 12 in the Chancery Division and 16 in the Family Division.

The High Court has its headquarters at the Royal Courts of Justice in the Strand in London, but for the convenience of litigants and their solicitors there are a number of district registries in the larger cities in England and Wales. It is thus possible for cases to be dealt with at the Crown Court in certain provincial cities so avoiding the need to take the parties and witnesses to London.

Inevitably the administration of the courts call for a large number of administrative staff of varying degrees of seniority to organise the lists of cases for the judges and also to deal with the day to day work of the Divisions of the High Court. The senior administrators of the Central Office of the Supreme Court in London are eleven Masters in the Queen's Bench Division, six Chancery Masters and four Registrars in Bankruptcy in the Chancery Division and 14 Registrars in the Family Division.

The Queen's Bench Division

This, the great common law court, takes its name from the fact that the early royal judges sat on "the bench"—*in banc*—at Westminster. As a result of the reconstruction of the courts in the Judicature Acts 1873–1875, and the transfer to the Queen's Bench Division in 1880 of the jurisdiction of the Common Pleas and Exchequer Divisions, this court has absorbed the whole common law jurisdiction. The present jurisdiction of the Division is thus both civil and criminal, original and appellate.

In terms of its civil jurisdiction, with which this chapter is particularly concerned, this can be simply stated as all cases in contract and tort whatever the value of the claim. In practice the court will normally take cases only if the amount claimed is above the county court limit of £5,000. This will include all substantial actions for damages arising from motor-vehicle accidents, or from accidents at work, so that it is hardly surprising that this Division has the largest allocation of High Court judges and hears by far the largest number of High Court cases. Cases are heard in London or at the Crown Court. One branch within the Division is the Commerical Court, where five Queen's Bench Division judges with special commercial experience hear cases of a commercial nature, concerning insurance, banking and the interpretation of mercantile documents like negotiable instruments or bills of lading. The procedure is deliberately kept informal and the strict rules relating to documents and evidence are relaxed.

An addition to the civil functions of the Queen's Bench Division under the Administration of Justice Act 1970 was the transfer to it of the Admiralty work of the former Probate Divorce and Admiralty Division. As with the Commercial Court, a separate Admiralty Court with its own judge has been established.

As well as these various responsibilities five judges are appointed to hear cases in the Restrictive Practices Court, which was created by Parliament under the Restrictive Trade Practices Act 1956. Under these statutory arrangements, one judge with two specially appointed laymen form the court to hear a case. A similar arrangement applies to the Employment Appeal Tribunal which hears appeals from Industrial Tribunals.

In its criminal jurisdiction the Queen's Bench Division furnishes the judges who try, with a jury, the most serious criminal offences at the Crown Court throughout England and Wales (see p. 60). It seems that in general terms a judge spends half his time on circuit and half his time in London. However, some of the cases dealt with at the Crown Court will be civil in nature, so it does not follow that the judge's time is evenly divided between civil and criminal work.

The Queen's Bench Divisional Court

In its appellate jurisdiction the Queen's Bench, like the other two Divisions, has what is rather confusingly called, a Divisional Court. This is, in most instances, an appeal court of at least two, but possibly three judges, and in the case of the Queen's Bench Divisional Court has the following jurisdiction:

  (i) It hears appeals in summary criminal cases on a point of law by way of case stated from the decisions of the magistrates in their court of summary jurisdiction, or from a summary case appeal tried in the Crown Court. This is dealt with more fully at page 57 in the next chapter.
 (ii) It hears an appeal by a solicitor against a determination of the Solicitors' Disciplinary Tribunal.
(iii) It exercises the supervisory jurisdiction of the High Court over inferior courts and tribunals. Judges of the divisional court regularly hear applications for the prerogative writ of habeas corpus and the prerogative orders of certiorari, mandamus and prohibition. These orders are of general value as a method by which the courts can exercise control over inferior courts, tribunals and public officials. The writ of habeas

corpus orders a person's detention to be brought before the court to be justified. It thus prevents unlawful imprisonment. The order of certiorari quashes unlawful decisions by inferior courts and tribunals. The order of mandamus instructs a public body to carry out its statutory public duty in accordance with the law. The order of prohibition requires an inferior court or tribunal to stop hearing a case which is in excess of its jurisdiction. These orders are dealt with more fully at page 104 below.

The Chancery Division

This Division is the direct descendant of the Lord Chancellor's equity jurisdiction (see Chapter 14), and it is thus substantially concerned with those matters which before the Judicature Acts 1873–1875 belonged to the Court of Chancery. It has also had allocated to it by statute the responsibility for such important matters as the winding-up of companies and revenue cases. Its jurisdiction can be summarised as:

the execution of trusts;
the redemption and foreclosure of mortgages;
partnership actions;
the administration of the estates of deceased persons;
the rectification and cancellation of deeds;
specific performance of contracts for the sale or lease of interests in land;
conveyancing and land law matters;
patent, trade mark, registered design or copyright actions
revenue matters, *i.e.* taxation cases;
company law matters.

An addition to the Chancery Division jurisdiction, under the Administration of Justice Act 1970, was the hearing of contentious probate cases where litigation is involved. Under the same Act the wardship of minors was transferred from the Chancery Division to the Family Division.

Many of the cases which come before a Chancery Division judge are not disputes, so much as a proposed course of action which calls for judicial approval. This is often the case when executors or administrators seek approval to a distribution arrangement for a deceased person's estate, or when arrangements need to be approved for altering a company's structure.

The 12 Chancery judges are presided over nominally by the Lord Chancellor, but this is for historical reasons and in practice he does not sit. Instead the Vice-Chancellor heads the Division. Most Chancery cases are heard at the Royal Courts of Justice in London without a jury. It is possible for cases to be tried at eight designated provincial first-tier centres. Because of the specialised nature of Chancery work there is a separate Chancery Bar for the barristers who practice in the Chancery Division, and it is from this group of barristers that new Chancery Division judges are appointed. Chancery barristers usually have chambers in Lincoln's Inn. The six Chancery Masters are solicitors, and they assist the judges to draw up the often complex court orders. They can, if so required, take the complicated accounts which are frequently involved in Chancery actions.

The Chancery Divisional Court
The Chancery Divisional Court may consist of one or two judges. It hears certain income tax appeals from the Commissioners of Inland Revenue and it also hears appeals from county courts in bankruptcy and land registration matters. The total of cases heard in 1985 was 58.

The Family Division
This Division of the High Court came into being under provisions contained in the Administration of Justice Act 1970. It retains the jurisdiction in matrimonial causes previously vested in its predecessor the Probate, Divorce and Admiralty Division, and it has also been given the former Chancery Division jurisdiction over wardship proceedings and other matters concerning minors. The Division is headed by a President who has 16 High Court judges to assist him.

The main responsibilities of the Family Division are:

  (i) the grant of legal title—probate or letters of administration—to authorise named executors or administrators to wind up a deceased person's estate. This work is done at the Principal Registry in London, or at a number of district registries in various cities of England and Wales;
 (ii) the hearing of defended or complex divorce and matrimonial cases, either in London or at certain designated provincial centres. All matters relevant to the case, such as maintenance for the wife, or custody of the children, are also dealt with;
(iii) applications relating to legitimacy, validity of marriage, presumption of death, adoption, guardianship, wardship, and custody of minors, consent to marriage of a minor, title to property in a dispute between spouses, and in particular

where a spouse continues in occupation of a dwelling-house as the matrimonial home.

The Family Divisional Court

The Family Divisional Court consists of two judges and hears appeals from decisions of magistrates, the county court and the Crown Court in family law matters, for example, decisions concerning affiliation orders on a point of law by case stated; decisions relating to adoption orders; and finally decisions in domestic proceedings, such as the making of maintenance orders. The total of appeals in 1985 was 134.

Appeals

An appeal from the decision of a judge sitting in any one of the three Divisions of the High Court will go the Court of Appeal (Civil Division).

The one exception to this rule, introduced by the Administration of Justice Act 1969, is that it is possible for an appeal to "leapfrog" the Court of Appeal and go direct to the House of Lords provided:

(i) the trial judge is prepared to grant a certificate;
(ii) the parties agree to this course;
(iii) a point of law of general public importance is involved, which relates wholly or mainly to the construction of a statute or statutory instrument; or the judge was bound by a previous decision of the Court of Appeal or the House of Lords; and
(iv) the House of Lords grants leave.

In view of these stringent conditions not many successful applications are made. A recent example of a leap-frog appeal is *President of India* v. *La Pintada Compania* (1985) which was concerned with the payment of interest on a debt paid late. The High Court Judge had found himself bound by earlier Court of Appeal decisions.

4. Court of Appeal (Civil Division)

The Court of Appeal was created by the Judicature Acts 1873–1875 together with the High Court of Justice to form the Supreme Court of Judicature. It was at first intended that the Court of Appeal should be the final appeal court, but a change of plan led to the Appellate Jurisdiction Act 1876, under which the House of Lords in its judicial capacity was retained as the supreme appeal court.

A special group of judges called Lords Justices of Appeal were appointed to form the Court of Appeal in civil cases. At first there were five but the present number is 22.

Originally appeals came only from the five Divisions of the High Court, but since 1934 appeals from the county court have also come to the Court of Appeal. The present jurisdiction of the court includes appeals from the three Divisions of the High Court, including divisional courts, from the county courts, from the Employment Appeal Tribunal, from the Lands Tribunal and the Transport Tribunal.

The Master of the Rolls is, in practice, the senior judge of the Court of Appeal (Civil Division), although the Lord Chancellor, ex-Lord Chancellors, the Lord Chief Justice, the President of the Family Division the Vice Chancellor and the Lords of Appeal in Ordinary are all members of the court. Three judges usually sit to form a court but in a case of great importance (see *Ward* v. *James* (1966), p. 36 a "full court" of five judges is possible. It will be obvious from the number of judges that the Court of Appeal (Civil Division) will sit in four or five Divisions on any one day. This explains the fact that in an average year this court will actually hear nearly 1,000 cases. Of these about a third will come on appeal from the county court.

Since the Criminal Appeal Act 1966 the Court of Appeal has had a Criminal Division, replacing the former Court of Criminal Appeal. It is presided over by the Lord Chief Justice who with two other judges hears a wide range of appeals in criminal cases (see p. 61). Both Divisions sit only at the Royal Courts of Justice in London.

In civil appeals the appellant has six weeks from the date of the judgment of the court below, in which to give the Court of Appeal a formal notice of appeal, specifying the exact grounds on which the court will be asked to say that the trial judge or the jury went wrong in the lower court. Although the appeal is "by way of rehearing" there is no question of a full rehearing in the Court of Appeal; full legal argument is heard but no witnesses are called and the court is only concerned to give a ruling on the point of law in dispute. Further evidence may be given to the Court of Appeal but the court will only exercise its powers to receive such evidence in restricted circumstances.

Court of Appeal (Civil Division)

	'82	'83	'84	'85
Appeals disposed of by judgment after a hearing	966	898	975	989

5. House of Lords

The House of Lords in its judicial capacity is the final court of appeal in matters civil and criminal from all courts in England, Wales and Northern Ireland; and in matters civil from courts in Scotland. It first assumed its present jurisdiction under the Appellate Jurisdiction Act 1876 but whereas there was then provision for two judges, there is now a maximum of 11 Lords of Appeal in Ordinary—known as the Law Lords—to try these appeals. At least one of the judges will be from Scotland and one from Northern Ireland. In addition to the Lords of Appeal in Ordinary other judges who can take part in the work of the House are the Lord Chancellor, ex-Lord Chancellors, the Master of the Rolls and peers who have held high judicial office. By a convention lay peers do not take part in the hearing of appeals.

The court, for which a quorum is three, normally has five judges sitting to hear the appeal. The case is heard in a committee room of the House of Lords at Westminster. The judges wear lounge suits, although counsel are in wigs and robes, and the atmosphere is comparatively informal. The cases heard always raise a point of law of general public importance, which is the sole ground for obtaining leave to appeal to the House of Lords. In English appeals the leave of the court below, which may be the Court of Appeal (Civil Division), the Court of Appeal (Criminal Division) or the Queen's Bench Divisional Court when dealing with a point of law in a case stated from a magistrates' court or with a judicial review, is necessary. If leave is refused by the court below, it is still possible for a party wishing to appeal to ask the Appeal Committee of the House of Lords itself to give leave to appeal. An alternative source of appeal cases, introduced by the Administration of Justice Act 1969, allows a High Court judge, in certain defined circumstances, to grant a certificate to a party that in his view the House of Lords should consider the case. If the Appeal Committee of the House of Lords agree with the judge the appeal will "leapfrog" the Court of Appeal. All parties to the proceedings must consent to the grant of the certificate and the appeal must be on a point of law either concerning the construction of a statute or statutory instrument which has been both fully argued and fully considered in the judgment in the proceedings, or concerning a precedent of the House of Lords or the Court of Appeal by which the judge was bound.

The court after hearing the appeal case argued by counsel will take time to prepare its judgment. This is shown at the conclusion of the Law Report by the Latin words *"Curia advisari vult"*—the court wishes to consider the matter. It is open to all five judges to give individual speeches and then the majority view prevails. The court finally give notice of their decision to the House of Lords itself, so that the judgment can be formally recorded. Judgments of the House of Lords are almost always reported, because every one adds some new principle to, or clarifies some existing principle of, law. As the supreme court the decisions of the House of Lords are binding on all lower courts, and they thus form an important element as a source of law in connection with the doctrine of judicial precedent (see page 126).

Number of appeals disposed of by judgment after a hearing from:	'81	'82	'83	'84	'85
Court of Appeal (Civil division)	47	45	44	39	41
Court of Appeal (Criminal division)	5	11	11	6	8
Queen's Bench Divisional Court	7	14	7	8	5
High Court (Leapfrog)	4	2	2	3	1
Scotland Court of Session	9	7	9	3	3
Northern Ireland Courts of	2	0	3	3	0
Total:	74	79	76	62	58

6. The European Court of Justice

The European Communities Act 1972 set the seal on the United Kingdom's entry to what was more familiarly known at the time as the Common Market. In passing the legislation Parliament accepted that, in the interpretation of the various Treaties between the Member States of the Community, the supreme court for deciding disputes would be the European Court of Justice.

In *H. P. Bulmer Ltd.* v. *J. Bollinger S.A.* (1974) Lord Denning M.R. explained the position with characteristic clarity:

> "the Treaty concerns only those matters which have a European element, that is to say, matters which affect people or property in the nine countries of the Common Market besides

The Structure of the Civil Courts

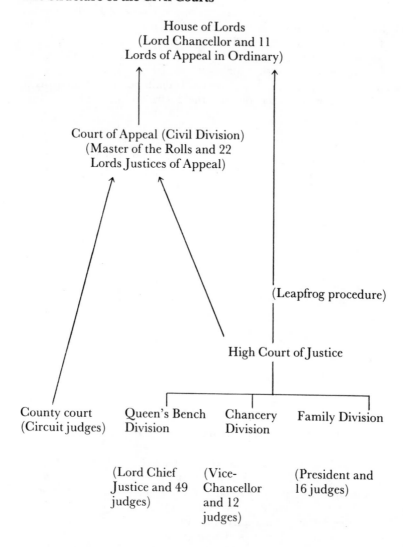

House of Lords
(Lord Chancellor and 11
Lords of Appeal in Ordinary)

Court of Appeal (Civil Division)
(Master of the Rolls and 22
Lords Justices of Appeal)

(Leapfrog procedure)

High Court of Justice

County court   Queen's Bench   Chancery   Family Division
(Circuit judges)   Division   Division

(Lord Chief   (Vice-   (President and
Justice and 49   Chancellor   16 judges)
judges)   and 12
                     judges)

ourselves. The Treaty does not touch any of the matters which concern solely England and the people in it. These are still governed by English law. They are not affected by the Treaty. But when we come to matters with a European element the Treaty is like an incoming tide. It flows into the estuaries and up the

rivers. It cannot be held back . . . . In the task of interpreting
the Treaty, the English judges are no longer the final authority. . . . The supreme tribunal for interpreting the Treaty is
the European Court of Justice at Luxembourg."

The European Court of Justice consists currently of 13 judges,
each of whom is an eminent judge in his own country and who is
appointed for a six-year term by the governments of the Member
States. The judges are assisted by six Advocates-General who prepare reasoned conclusions on the cases submitted to the court. The
court is not bound by judicial precedent and has a flexible approach
to the interpretation of the Treaties.

7. The European Commission of Human Rights

In 1950 the United Kingdom was an original signatory to the European Convention on Human Rights which was established under
the auspices of the Council of Europe. It is possible for subjects of
the United Kingdom dissatisfied with decisions of English courts to
petition the European Commission of Human Rights and for disputes ultimately to be heard by the Court of Human Rights which
sits at Strasbourg. Over the years the U.K. Government has been
found to be in breach of the Convention in various respects in 11 out
of 12 hearings. Changes in English law have followed.

8. Miscellaneous Civil Courts

Judicial Committee of the Privy Council
This Committee advises the Queen on appeals from the Isle of
Man, Channel Islands, Commonwealth countries and from certain
of the independent Commonwealth states. The Judicial Committee
is composed of Privy Councillors who have held or now hold high
judicial office. Each case must be heard by not more than five and
not less than three members of the Committee. In practice the court
usually consists of three or five Lords of Appeal in Ordinary, often
assisted by a senior judge from the country concerned. The decision,
or advice, of the Committee is given effect by an Order in Council.
The Committee also hears appeals from the ecclesiastical courts,
from prize courts (captured shipping), and from certain domestic
tribunals in England and Wales, such as decisions of the General
Medical Council, where professional men have been disciplined by
the tribunal. This latter jurisdiction is derived from statute. In 1985
the total of cases disposed of after a hearing was 48.

Ecclesiastical courts

These courts at the present time exercise control over clergymen of the Church of England. In each diocese there is a consistory court, the judge of which is a barrister appointed by the bishop, and known as the Chancellor. Appeal lies from the consistory court to, depending on the diocese, the Arches Court of Canterbury or the Chancery Court of York, and from either court a further appeal is possible to the Judicial Committee of the Privy Council.

Court of Protection

Under the Mental Health Act 1983 a judge of the Chancery Division can sit as a Court of Protection to administer the estate of a person of unsound mind.

Restrictive Practices Court

This court was set up by the Restrictive Trade Practices Act 1956 to examine agreements which restrict prices or the conditions of supply of goods. The court consists of one High Court judge and at least two lay members specially appointed. Appeal lies to the Court of Appeal. The court sat for four days in 1985.

The Coroner's Court

The Coroner's Court is used to inquire (by an inquest) into unexplained deaths which have occurred other than through natural causes. For certain inquests the coroner may, and sometimes must, call a jury of from seven to 11 persons to return a verdict as to the cause of death. The coroner must either be legally or medically qualified.

The Employment Appeal Tribunal

This court was established by the Employment Protection Act 1975 to hear appeals from decisions of Industrial Tribunals, in particular those relating to unfair dismissal, equal pay and redundancy. The composition of the court for a hearing is one High Court judge sitting with two laymen who have specialised knowledge of industrial relations. Appeals from the Employment Appeal Tribunal on points of law go direct to the Court of Appeal. In 1985 the court dealt with 459 appeals of which 382 concerned unfair dismissal.

6. Criminal Courts

1. The Criminal Court Structure

There is a basic division of crimes in the English legal system into summary criminal offences and indictable criminal offences. To complicate the matter, some summary offences can be tried like indictable cases, and many indictable offences can be tried summarily. These distinctions will have to be examined and explained later, but the English criminal court structure is based on the simple division into summary and indictable offences. This chapter will begin by studying the courts which may be involved where a summary offence is committed and then proceed to consider the quite different court structure which is provided to deal with indictable offences.

2. Summary Offences

Court of Summary Jurisdiction/magistrates' court

The court which has been provided by Parliament to try cases designated as summary is the local magistrates' court. This court is sometimes known by its old name of petty sessions and sometimes by its formal title of court of summary jurisdiction. At one time it was also known as the police court but one hopes that this title is no longer widely used, since it conveys the impression that the court sits at the convenience of the police to distribute punishment in accordance with police evidence. As the police inevitably figure prominently in the magistrates' court, it is not surprising that the public has tended to think of it as the police court. It is vital to the administration of justice that the magistrates should consistently endeavour to make it clear to persons appearing before them that they have no bias in the case. To this end it is desirable that the staff of the court, like ushers and messengers, should be local authority employees who have obviously no connection with the police. The point is worth labouring because at some time in their lives the vast majority of people will be required as defendants, or as witnesses, to attend a magistrates' court. The impression which they form on that occasion will condition their whole future attitude to the administration of justice. In this sense of the number of ordinary people affected, the importance of fair procedure and unbiased trial before magistrates is of greater importance even than the much more solemn course taken in criminal trials of indictable offences where judge and jury are concerned.

Summary offences are offences which Parliament has specifically named as being suitable for trial before local magistrates. Thus all summary offences are statutorily defined. In general terms they consist of offences which can be treated as of minor importance. Some of them, like certain Road Traffic Act offences, are really particular forms of misconduct which are only criminal in the widest sense of that term. Amongst other common summary offences are minor thefts such as shoplifting, minor assaults and drunkenness in a public place. These are only the prime examples of a vast number of summary offences known to the law; to obtain a better idea of the scope of the magistrates' full jurisdiction reference should be made to an annual publication known as Stone's *Justices' Manual*. This work in three volumes now runs into several thousand pages. Even a cursory examination of its Table of Contents reveals the enormous range of summary offences which can fall to the magistrates for determination.

The appointment of magistrates has been considered in Chapter 3, but so far as the court structure is concerned the local magistrates' court is the lowest rung of the ladder. Every person who is charged with having committed a summary offence will have his case brought before the magistrates in the magistrates' court for the locality where the offence has been committed. In many instances it is necessary for the accused to be present at the hearing because the court may wish to see him and it does have power to send him to prison. On the other hand, for certain Road Traffic Act offences, it is possible for the accused to plead guilty by post and save himself the need to attend court.

For the hearing the magistrates' court will usually consist of from two to seven lay magistrates forming "the bench" and they have powers dependent upon the statute which applies to the case, but at the maximum these allow them to send an offender to prison for up to six months and/or impose a fine of up to £2,000. If the person concerned is convicted of two or more offences at the same time, the maximum sentence of imprisonment goes up to 12 months. If, after conviction, on hearing the record of the person convicted the bench feel that their powers of sentence are inadequate, they may commit that person to the Crown Court for the locality so that a higher sentence can be given by that court. Where a stipendiary magistrate takes the place of lay magistrates, he has, sitting alone, the same powers as a bench of magistrates.

At the hearing of a summary case, the bench of magistrates have the assistance of the "clerk to the justices" or magistrates' clerk. He is legally qualified, usually as a solicitor, and he is present to advise the magistrates on the law applicable to the case and to control the administration of the court. He must, however, be careful not to give the impression that he is the most important person in the court, and he must not therefore retire with the magistrates, nor offer legal advice until it is asked for, unless the magistrates are failing to appreciate a legal issue. It is not an easy role but it is an important one, since the successful combination of the lay magistrates with the legally qualified clerk is fundamental to the success of the English legal system. It has been estimated that, in total, magistrates deal with 97 per cent. of criminal cases.

As was stated at the outset, magistrates hear not only cases which must be tried summarily but also certain offences which are triable "either way." This procedure is dealt with in detail in the Magistrates Courts Act 1980 and is considered in Chapter 7. The result of this legislation is that, in practice, the magistrates deal with a large number of indictable offences. The same procedure is followed as for offences which are triable summarily only.

Special considerations apply where the accused person is a juvenile, because by statute special arrangements are made for trial by magistrates in juvenile courts. The intention is to take cases concerning children and young persons away from the publicity of the ordinary courts and allow them to be dealt with privately by the magistrates.

The Crown Court

If a person who has been convicted by the magistrates of a summary offence wishes to appeal, he has two courses open to him. He can appeal on the facts of the case to the Crown Court for the area where the case has been heard, or, if his appeal is concerned with a specific point of law, then he can appeal to the Queen's Bench Divisional Court.

The difference between appealing on fact or law is perhaps best understood from an example. If the prosecution is for the offence of exceeding the authorised speed limit, and there is a conflict between the evidence of the police witnesses and that of the driver and his passenger as to the speed of the vehicle over the given distance, then that is an argument about fact, and an appeal against conviction made by the driver would go to the Crown Court. If, however, the charge is of driving whilst under the influence of drink, and the driver argues that the breathalyser equipment used by the police was not of an approved type, then that is a point of law and an appeal based on it would go to the Queen's Bench Divisional Court. Where the defendant pleaded not guilty in the magistrates' court he may appeal to the Crown Court against both conviction and sentence: if he pleaded guilty he may only appeal against sentence.

The composition of the Crown Court varies depending upon whether it is dealing with a summary appeal case or an indictable trial with a jury. For a summary appeal case it is usual for either a circuit judge or a recorder to sit and he must be accompanied by not less than two nor more than four magistrates. The decision of the court is by a majority and the regular judge has a second and casting vote if the members are equally divided. Naturally the magistrates must accept the regular judge's pronouncements on matters of law. The magistrates will also sit with the regular judge to deal with persons who have been convicted by a magistrates' court and who have been committed for sentence to the Crown Court.

In its appeal court role the Crown Court holds a complete rehearing of the case. This means that a second trial takes place, since the parties and the witnesses all give their evidence again. The Crown Court then reaches its own independent conclusion. No jury is used in these appeal cases and there is no further appeal possible on fact in a summary case from the Crown Court. If on the appeal a point of law is argued before the court, it may, having given its own decision, agree to state a case for the consideration of the Queen's Bench Divisional Court. This corresponds to the practice of magistrates stating such cases where the point of law arises in a summary case in the magistrates' court.

Queen's Bench Divisional Court

As has just been seen, an appeal on a point of law from the magistrates' court's decision or the decision of the Crown Court is heard by the Queen's Bench Divisional Court. This court sits only in the Royal Courts of Justice in London and consists of two or three Queen's Bench Division judges. The process by which the appeal is brought is known as a case stated. This means that the convicted person, or his legal representative, asks the magistrates, when they have decided the point of law against him, to state a case for the consideration of the Queen's Bench Divisional Court. This case is then prepared in writing by the clerk to the justices setting out the point of law which was raised, the decision of the magistrates and the reason why they decided it as they did. One unusual feature of the appeal provisions is that it is open to the prosecutor to ask the magistrates to state a case for the consideration of the Divisional Court, where the magistrates have ruled on the point of law in favour of the person accused. This is only so on a point of law; the prosecutor cannot appeal against the magistrates' finding on the facts.

The arguments over the use of the breathalyser are good examples of instances where a number of appeals by case stated have gone to the Divisional Court. All of these turned on law and not on fact. Another example is *Hall* v. *Hyder* (1966) where the point of law was whether a licensee who sells a shandy to a person under age is supplying "intoxicating liquor" or not. The court, presided over by the Lord Chief Justice, held that the sale of a shandy involves the sale of beer, which is an intoxicating liquor, and the offence was thus committed!

If the Divisional Court decides that the magistrates were wrong, it has three options open to it: (i) it may reverse or amend the magistrates' decision; (ii) it may remit the case to the magistrates requiring them either to continue hearing the case, or to discharge or convict the accused, or to hold a fresh hearing before another bench of magistrates, as appropriate; (iii) it may make such other order as seems just. In 1985 the court dealt with 193 appeals by case stated.

As will be obvious, legal rulings given by the court are of very considerable consequence to the police, and to the magistrates and their clerks.

The Queen's Bench Divisional Court also supervises the functioning of magistrates' courts and the Crown Court in their dealings with summary cases. The use of the prerogative orders in the exercise of this supervision is considered at page 104 below.

House of Lords

Where the case stated raises a point of law of general public importance, provided leave is given by the Queen's Bench Divisional Court or by the Appeal Committee of the House of Lords, an appeal is possible by either the prosecution or the defence to the House of Lords. This has been so since 1960 but originally very few appeals were heard. The annual number has increased in recent years. An example from 1985 is *Wings Ltd.* v. *Ellis* (1985) in which a travel company in a brochure indicated that a hotel had air conditioning when it did not. Although the company published a correction, a customer booked a holiday relying on the brochure and unaware of the amendment. Had the company committed an offence under the Trade Descriptions Act 1968? The House of Lords held that it had.

Diagram of Criminal Court Structure for Summary Offences

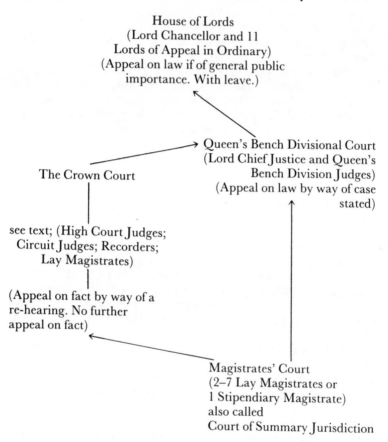

House of Lords
(Lord Chancellor and 11
Lords of Appeal in Ordinary)
(Appeal on law if of general public
importance. With leave.)

Queen's Bench Divisional Court
(Lord Chief Justice and Queen's
Bench Division Judges)
(Appeal on law by way of case
stated)

The Crown Court

see text; (High Court Judges;
Circuit Judges; Recorders;
Lay Magistrates)

(Appeal on fact by way of a
re-hearing. No further
appeal on fact)

Magistrates' Court
(2–7 Lay Magistrates or
1 Stipendiary Magistrate)
also called
Court of Summary Jurisdiction

Where an appeal does reach the House of Lords, it is heard and determined by five Lords of Appeal in Ordinary, as in other civil and criminal appeals at this final level. It is not surprising that so few summary cases are heard by the House of Lords, because in the vast majority of such cases the arguments are entirely on fact, and it will only be on rare occasions that a point of law of substance emerges.

In recent years Queen's Bench Divisional Court appeals actually heard by the House of Lords have numbered:

1981   7
1982   14
1983   7
1984   8
1985   5

3. Indictable Offences

As has been seen some confusion can arise because, as well as certain criminal offences which can only be tried on indictment, the Magistrates Courts Act 1980 designates certain other offences as "either way" offences. This means that depending on the particular facts such a case may either be sent for trial on indictment or be tried summarily (see page 72).

Indictable offences are recognised at common law, or by statute, and are generally the more serious forms of crime. All forms of homicide, major theft, assaults inflicting bodily harm, rape, and perjury are examples of the sort of matters with which this section of the chapter is concerned.

The word "indictment" means a document which sets out in writing the charges against the accused person. Each separate charge is called "a count" of the indictment.

Examining magistrates' procedure

Where a person is accused of an indictable offence the first stage in the court system with which he will be concerned is the examining magistrates' procedure. What this means is that before there is any question of a trial, the prosecutor must be able to satisfy the magistrates that he has an adequate case to warrant the magistrates sending the accused person for trial.

At the examining magistrates' proceedings two magistrates usually sit, with the clerk to the justices, to hear the prosecution present its case against the accused either in full or, with the consent of the defence, by documentary evidence. A record is taken of the evidence given by the prosecution witnesses and at the end of the hearing the magistrates decide if there is a case to answer or not. The defence, although present, is not required to make any contribution, and it is customary for the legal representative of the accused "to reserve his defence" if the magistrates decide to commit the case for trial. The magistrates' decision is not the result of a trial because, it will be observed, they are only concerned with one side of the case. If satisfied that there is a prima facie case the magistrates commit the accused for trial, if on the other hand they are not satisfied they discharge him. In the latter event the prosecution can always return later with fresh evidence and ask the magistrates again to commit for trial.

The Crown Court

If the magistrates decide to commit the accused for trial the case will be put in the list for the Crown Court which sits to hear cases from that locality. There are some 90 court centres.

The Courts Act 1971 which abolished the courts of quarter sessions and assizes created in their place the Crown Court. The Crown Court forms part of the Supreme Court and under the 1971 Courts Act England and Wales are divided into six regions based on London, Bristol, Birmingham, Manchester, Cardiff and Leeds. Two High Court judges are appointed to each circuit and they are responsible for the organisational arrangements for the Crown Court. In addition they will themselves sit to try the most serious indictable cases. Below the two High Court judges in each region there are a number of circuit judges and a number of part-time recorders. Within the region certain towns are designated as having facilities for the trial of all cases, both civil and criminal. Other towns may be designated for all criminal cases, whilst others again may be limited to criminal cases tried by a circuit judge. The Lord Chancellor's department has, under the 1971 Act taken over responsibility for all the administrative arrangements involved. It should be noted that the Crown Court is a single entity; sittings of it take place as circumstances require.

From what has been said it will be evident that, theoretically, the trial of an indictable case can take place before (i) a High Court judge and jury or (ii) a circuit judge and jury or (iii) a recorder and jury. Lay magistrates may also sit with the circuit judge or the recorder (see above p. 31).

By a Practice Direction issued in October 1971 the Lord Chief Justice directed that offences should be classified into one of four categories and should be tried accordingly:

Class 1:   by a High Court judge only—for example, treason, offences resulting in death, serious breaches of the Official Secrets legislation; and incitement to these.

Class 2:   by a High Court judge unless released by him to a circuit judge or a recorder—for example, manslaughter, rape, mutiny, piracy, sexual offences against children; and incitement to these.

Class 3:   by a High Court judge or by a circuit judge or by a recorder—all indictable offences other than those falling within classes 1, 2 and 4.

Class 4:   normally by a circuit judge or by a recorder but can be by
           a High Court judge.

At the time the Courts Act 1971 was passed the intention was that
an accused person should not have to wait more than eight weeks
between committal and trial. Because of the increase in crime it has
not been possible to meet this objective. The waiting period outside
London is about 15 weeks for those on bail and ten weeks for those in
custody; and in London the waiting period is about 26 weeks for
those on bail, 17 weeks for those in custody.

The Prosecution of Offences Act 1985 has introduced the concept
of time limits in the use of custody and in the institution of criminal
proceedings in an attempt to remedy the situation. The Old Bailey,
or more properly the Central Criminal Court, operates as the central
Crown Court for London and deals with a massive annual case load.

As the court of first instance trying indictable cases the Crown
Court will call for the assistance of a jury of 12 whenever a "not
guilty" plea is entered. The High Court judge, circuit judge or
recorder, as the case may be, will direct the jury as to the law and
will ensure that the case is conducted in accordance with proper procedure. After the jury has returned its verdict of "guilty" or "not
guilty" the judge is responsible in the former case for sentencing the
prisoner and in the latter for discharging him.

An appeal from the Crown Court against conviction and/or sentence can be made to the Court of Appeal (Criminal Division).
Notice has to be given or the application made within 28 days of the
conviction or sentence complained of.

It is necessary to reiterate that the Crown Court also has civil jurisdiction in that the High Court judges can try civil High Court
actions and the circuit judges can, and do, act as county court
judges. Since the Courts Act 1971 it is even possible for a Chancery
action to be heard in certain designated cities outside London.

Court of Appeal (Criminal Division)

The Court of Appeal (Criminal Division) was established under
the provisions of the Criminal Appeal Act 1966 to replace the former
Court of Criminal Appeal. The law which governs the court is now
to be found in the Criminal Appeal Act 1968.

The Court of Appeal (Criminal Division) sits only at the Royal
Courts of Justice in London but it usually sits in three divisions. The
court is made up of the Lord Chief Justice, Lords Justices of Appeal
and a number of Queen's Bench Division judges specially nomi-
nated by the Lord Chief Justice. At least three judges must sit—and
the number is not usually more—for the hearing of an appeal.

Generally these will be the Lord Chief Justice, one Lord Justice of Appeal and one Queen's Bench Division judge; but if the Lord Chief Justice is not available, the court can take the form of two Lords Justices of Appeal and one Queen's Bench Division judge, or one Lord Justice of Appeal and two Queen's Bench Division judges, or even three Queen's Bench Division judges.

The jurisdiction of the Court of Appeal (Criminal Division) is

(i)   to hear appeals against conviction on indictment where the grounds of appeal involve a question of law, and to hear appeals against conviction where the court grants leave and where the grounds of appeal involve a question of fact alone, or a question of mixed law and fact or any other ground which the court regards as sufficient. Alternatively the trial judge can grant a certificate that the case, being one of fact or mixed law and fact, justifies an appeal.

(ii) to hear appeals against sentence pronounced by the Crown Court provided that the sentence is not one fixed by law and provided that the court grants leave. An application for leave may be determined by a single judge, but if he refuses leave the appellant can require a full court, *i.e.* two or more judges to determine the matter.

(iii) to hear cases referred to it by the Home Secretary. Cases may be referred in full or the court's view may be sought on a particular aspect of the case.

(iv) to hear appeals against a verdict of "not guilty by reason of insanity" or against findings of fitness and unfitness to plead.

(v)   to hear an appeal by the prosecution against an acquittal on a point of law at the trial in the Crown Court. This provision involves an application by the Attorney-General for the opinion of the court on the point of law. The result cannot affect the acquittal and the defendant is not named in the appeal.

A proposed new responsibility is for the court to give guidelines in sentencing, particularly where anxiety has been expressed about an unduly lenient sentence.

The Court of Appeal (Criminal Division) on the hearing of an appeal has wide statutory powers to deal with the matter. In regard to a conviction it has power to quash the conviction when "under all the circumstances of the case the verdict is unsafe or unsatisfactory" or it may do so where the judgment of the court should be set aside on the ground of a wrong decision on any question of law or where there was a material irregularity in the course of the trial, *e.g.* undue interruption by the judge. It is necessary to observe that even where an appeal may technically succeed the court can "apply the proviso" and order the conviction to stand. This is because the court is entitled to take the view that a reasonable jury after a proper summing up would still have convicted the defendant so that no miscarriage of justice has actually occurred.

Where the appeal is against the sentence imposed the court can reduce or vary the sentence but it has no power to increase it.

On procedural grounds the court can order a new trial if it considers that the interests of justice so require, or it may order a *venire de novo*, which amounts to a new trial, because the previous trial was so irregular as to amount to a nullity.

House of Lords

Because the House of Lords is the supreme court of appeal for civil and criminal cases in the English legal system, a final appeal to it from the decision of the Court of Appeal (Criminal Division) is possible. An appeal can be brought by either the prosecution or the defence, if the Court of Appeal grants leave to appeal and certifies that a point of law of general public importance is involved, and that the point ought to be considered by the House of Lords. If the Court of Appeal refuses leave to appeal, but certifies that a point of law of general public importance is involved, then the appellant can ask the Appeal Committee of the House of Lords to grant leave to appeal. If leave is not given no appeal can be brought.

Until the Administration of Justice Act 1960, an appeal from the Court of Criminal Appeal to the House of Lords could only be brought by the appellant first obtaining the "fiat" of the Attorney-General.

Leave to appeal is not lightly given, and the House of Lords is hardly overburdened with appeals from the Court of Appeal (Criminal Division) as the following figures show.

1981	5
1982	11
1983	11
1984	6
1985	8

For the hearing of an appeal the court is made up of five Lords of Appeal in Ordinary.

4. Courts Martial

A special type of criminal court is the Court Martial which is used to enforce the law applicable to the armed forces on service personnel. It is thus a criminal court, in the sense that many of the cases within its jurisdiction concern conduct which would be an offence if committed by non-service personnel. Theft is an obvious example. Offences such as treason, murder, manslaughter or rape must be tried in the ordinary courts if committed in the United Kingdom. A court martial is composed of a small group of serving officers and in important cases the court will be advised by a judge advocate, who is a legally qualified serving officer.

Diagram of Criminal Court Structure for Indictable Offences

House of Lords
(Lord Chancellor and 11
Lords of Appeal in Ordinary)
(With leave)

↑

Court of Appeal (Criminal Division)
(Lord Chief Justice and Lords Justices
of Appeal and Queen's Bench Division
Judges. See text.)

↑

The Crown Court
(see text; High Court Judges;
Circuit Judges; Recorders;
Lay Magistrates)
(trial by jury)

↑

If reveals prima
facie case commit
for trial to

↑

Examining Magistrates'
Procedure
(2 Lay Magistrates or
1 Stipendiary Magistrate)
also called Preliminary Inquiry
or Committal Proceedings.

Since 1951 there has been a special Courts Martial Appeal Court to hear, as the name indicates, appeals from a person convicted and/or sentenced by a court martial. The appeal court has the same composition as the Court of Appeal (Criminal Division). From its decision it is possible, with leave, to appeal to the House of Lords; but this is very rare. Less than one case a year from this source reaches the House of Lords. Inevitably the case would have to raise a point of law of general public importance.

7. Procedure

1. Adjective Law

Just as for trial purposes a different court structure applies, depending on whether the matter is civil or criminal, so there is a considerable difference in the procedure which is used. This chapter examines first the procedure employed in the civil courts, starting with the county court and progressing to the High Court and the appeal courts; it then considers the procedure followed in the criminal courts in both summary and indictable offences.

The term used to describe the law of practice and procedure is adjective law; it is contrasted with substantive law which is the law administered by the courts.

2. Civil Procedure

The county court

An ordinary action is begun in the county court by the plaintiff, the person bringing the claim, filing a request for a summons at the county court office on a form which sets out the names, addresses and descriptions of the parties, together with the nature and amount of the claim. The court office then gives the plaintiff a plaint note, which states the time and place of the return day, and at the same time it arranges for the defendant in the action to be served with a summons giving notice of the details of the claim, at least 21 days before the hearing, and with forms on which the defendant may state his defence or admit his liability. Alternatively he may use a separate document or may not reply at all.

The plaintiff can only bring his claim in the county court area where the defendant resides, or where the cause of action arose. He is thus limited as to locality in deciding to commence proceedings.

The defendant has several choices open to him. If he pays the whole amount claimed into court within 14 days the action is said to be "stayed"; if he pays less than the full amount within the 14 days the plaintiff has to decide whether to accept or reject that amount in settlement of his claim; another possibility is that the defendant will admit the claim and offer to pay by instalments, and again the plaintiff has to decide whether to accept or not; if the defendant has a defence, or a set-off or counterclaim, it will be for him to take steps to defend accordingly. As was seen in the section on the county courts the vast majority of cases do not come to trial, most claims being settled without a hearing.

On the return day specified the registrar will hold a "pre-trial review." If the defendant does not appear and has filed no admission or defence the registrar may enter judgment for the plaintiff. If there is a defence and the case is proceeding to trial the registrar fixes the date for the hearing and gives any necessary directions to assist the parties and the court.

If the case does proceed to a hearing, the trial will be by the county court judge, unless the claim is undefended or is for less than £500 when the registrar usually deals with the case. In theory it is possible for a jury of eight to be called, but in practice the calling of a jury for a county court claim is rare. The actual hearing of the case follows the usual form of the plaintiff presenting his case first, calling witnesses in support of his allegations, with the defendant then answering the claim, calling witnesses to support his defence. A party can be represented by a solicitor, or by counsel if he so chooses. The judge, or registrar, concludes the matter by giving judgment on the claim.

The comparative simplicity of the procedure is the result of the concept of the county court as a local court providing a quick and inexpensive remedy for minor civil claims.

A special procedure is available when the claim is for a debt or other liquidated demand and the plaintiff believes that there is no defence to his claim. This is called a default action and the plaintiff will obtain judgment in default without the need for a trial if the defendant fails to take appropriate steps to defend.

Another possible procedure is a reference to arbitration. This was introduced by the Administration of Justice Act 1973 for small claims, at present those not exceeding £500. The judge or the registrar or an outside arbitrator may be appointed to act as the arbitrator and the advantage of the process is that it will be quick, cheap, held in private and lack formality. It is intended that no costs will be awarded to either side so that the employment of lawyers to represent parties will be less likely. This is the latest attempt to provide a method of recovering a small claim without the cost of recovery amounting to more than the claim.

The general jurisdiction of the county courts is to be found expressed in the County Courts Act 1984 (as amended), whilst the statutory instrument, known as the County Court Rules 1981 (as amended), controls in detail the procedure which is to be observed in the courts. The practitioner's task is simplified by an annual publication, called the *County Court Practice*, and known as "the Green Book."

The High Court of Justice
(a) General

As was seen in the chapter on the structure of the civil courts, the High Court has three Divisions, each derived historically and each having a separate jurisdiction. As a result of this variety in responsibility there are considerable differences in the formal methods used to bring matters to trial before the court. The example which follows is of the most typical kind of action, being a substantial claim in contract or tort to be heard in the Queen's Bench Division. It must not be overlooked that an action brought, for example, in the Chancery Division might take a quite different course, and be the subject of a totally different terminology.

(b) Pleadings

A claim for damages above the county court limit resulting from a breach of contract or the commission of a tort is begun in the Queen's Bench Division of the High Court by the plaintiff, or his legal representative, issuing a Writ against the defendant. This Writ of Summons is obtained from the central office of the Supreme Court or from a District Registry. It is a formal summons from the Lord Chancellor to the named defendant, notifying him of the commencement of the action and requiring him to acknowledge service to the court within 14 days. The Writ may be indorsed with a Statement of Claim but usually the Writ is accompanied by a separate Statement of Claim which sets out in detail the basis of the plaintiff's case. This is a most important document and consequently is usually drawn up by counsel, the presentation of the claim in this form being a highly technical matter.

The Writ, having been authenticated by the court, is either served on the defendant in person or served by post or delivered personally to his address. If he fails to acknowledge service as required under the terms of the Writ, he is taken to be admitting the claim in full by his own default, and in such circumstances the plaintiff can apply for judgment in his favour. The actual acknowledgment of service is a formality by which the defendant is expected to signify his intention to defend the action. Assuming that the defendant does acknowledge service he must take steps to defend the action and, in particular, he must make arrangements to file a defence. This is a formal document which deals step by step with the allegations contained in the Statement of Claim. It is necessary for the Defence to answer the Statement of Claim paragraph by paragraph, since the court works from the assumption that anything not formally denied in the Defence is thereby admitted. The rules state that the Statement of Claim must be served within 14 days of the service of the Writ, and the Defence must then be filed with the court within 14 days of service of the Statement of Claim. In practice the time for filing the Defence is extended, because it is almost always necessary for counsel to prepare this document and he is not likely to be able to do so in 14 days. Often the defendant, or the plaintiff, will ask for Further and Better Particulars of the Statement of Claim, or the Defence, before proceeding to answer in documentary form.

It is possible that the defendant, as an integral part of the action, will wish to bring a Counterclaim against the plaintiff, or perhaps claim a Set-Off; this means that he claims to be owed money by the plaintiff, which he proposes to set-off against the plaintiff's claim. If this happens and a Counterclaim or Set-Off is filed with the Defence, the plaintiff, in turn, will have to proceed to file a Defence to Counterclaim. In fact the documentary battle can continue through several exchanges with such documents as a Reply, a Rejoinder and theoretically a Surrejoinder, a Rebutter and Surrebutter as possible, but virtually extinct, candidates.

The object of this documentary "war" is so that "the pleadings," as the documents are collectively known, shall define exactly what are the issues between the parties. The result of these exchanges will be that the judge will be able, by perusal of the pleadings to ascertain just where the parties agree and where they disagree about the claim in the case. This should make easier his task at the trial.

When the pleadings are complete the plaintiff takes out a Summons for Directions, which is heard by a Master, or District Registrar, in the presence of representatives of the parties. He deals with any matters outstanding relating to Discovery of Documents—both sides are required to produce all relevant documents for inspection—or Interrogatories—the formal asking of certain questions, the answers to which are recorded as relevant to the issue between the parties—and decide on the place and mode of trial. Thereafter the case can be set down for trial in the court lists.

If the plaintiff fails to pursue his claim actively against the defendant, or fails to set the action down for trial, the latter can, as a last resort, ask the court to dismiss the action for want of prosecution. Naturally the court exercises its discretion sparingly.

In some cases, the lengthy procedure necessary to ensure that a case does actually come to trial may be by-passed by the plaintiff proceeding for summary judgment (under Order 14 of the Rules of the Supreme Court which regulate all procedural matters in the High Court). Where a statement of claim has been served, and the plaintiff believes the defendant has no real defence, he may apply to a master (see p. 42) for summary judgment. If the master is satisfied, after having heard the facts of the plaintiff's case and such defence as the defendant chooses to make out, that there is a proper case he may either order that judgment be entered for the plaintiff forthwith (if there is no real defence) or, if it appears to him that there is an issue which should be tried, give the defendant leave to defend either with or without conditions.

(c) Costs

One of the unsolved problems of civil litigation is the costs of the case. It must never be overlooked that the value of the claim to the plaintiff can be completely overshadowed by the costs of the action. The added consideration is that in the English system whoever loses the case has to pay his own costs and the costs of the other side. Together, these may well total more than the claim. This is even more true if the decision at first instance is challenged on appeal, since the loser then will have four sets of costs to pay, and if the case should reach the House of Lords six sets of costs will be at stake. No wonder it is said that today the great corporations—local authorities, government departments, statutory undertakings and insurance companies in particular—and individuals who have a legal aid certificate, are the only parties who can safely afford to litigate!

It can hardly be satisfactory justice for the individual if a lawyer has to advise a client to settle a case because of the consequence in costs if that client should lose the case. Currently, it is estimated that nine out of ten cases are settled before trial. From the standpoint of the legal system too, this may not be satisfactory in that many cases which are settled raise an important point of law and therefore deserve in the public interest to be tried.

(d) Appeal procedure

Appeal lies from the county court to the Court of Appeal (Civil Division) without leave unless the amount at issue does not exceed one half of the county court limit. Leave is not necessary where the appeal is the result of an application for an injunction or where custody and access to children is involved. In 1985 338 appeals from the county court were heard in the Court of Appeal. The county court generally provides about a third of the total of appeals heard in the Court of Appeal (Civil Division).

From the three Divisions of the High Court of Justice, and from Divisional Courts in civil matters, appeals also go to the Court of Appeal (Civil Division). In 1985, 125 Chancery Division, 312 Queen's Bench Division and 89 Family Division appeals were heard by the Court of Appeal. The hearing in the Court of Appeal is not a complete re-trial since witnesses are not normally heard again. The appellant in furnishing notice of appeal must specify precisely the grounds for his appeal and he will be limited to arguing these before the court. The parties have six weeks from the judge's judgment to give notice of appeal. The appeal will be heard by three Lord Justices of Appeal in about six months from the time when the appeal was set down for hearing. The number of appeals is now such that there are five courts sitting every day in term.

A further appeal to the House of Lords is possible, but only if the Court of Appeal gives leave, or the House of Lords, by its Appeal Committee, itself gives leave. Only cases that raise points of law of outstanding public importance reach the House of Lords. Appeals from England and Wales actually heard by the House of Lords in civil matters in 1985 numbered 42. For a hearing five Lords of Appeal in Ordinary form a court.

As was seen at page 46 under the Administration of Justice Act 1969, it is possible for an appeal to go direct from the High Court to the House of Lords and so "leapfrog" the Court of Appeal! Such an appeal must have the approval of the parties and of the High Court judge, who can grant a certificate to that effect, and also leave of the Appeal Committee of the House of Lords itself. It can only take place where the case concerns the construction of a statute or statutory instrument, which has been fully considered in the judge's judgment, or is one in which the judge was bound by judicial precedent of a higher court.

3. Criminal Procedure

Summary offences

Over the years there has been an increasing tendency to pass the responsibility for trying criminal cases of a less serious nature to the lay magistrates. Parliament has designated these offences as summary, and in various pieces of legislation has fixed maximum penalties for the offences involved. Just how vast in scope this function has become can be seen from a glance at the "bible" of the magistrates' court—the three-volume annual publication of Stones' *Justices' Manual.*

The most obvious work of the magistrates in dealing with summary offences is their adjudication in (i) almost all Road Traffic Act offences; (ii) minor theft cases, as shoplifting; (iii) drunk and disorderly behaviour; (iv) minor assault; and (v) minor criminal damage cases. In a sense, to attempt to list cases is misleading because, although the above offences are the most common, there are hundreds more which could be subject to proceedings at a magistrates' court hearing.

A summary case is usually begun by an information being laid before a justice of the peace for him to issue a summons to the person accused. The summons will require that person to appear at a named magistrates' court, at a time stipulated, so that the case against him may be heard. Prosecutions are now a matter for the Crown Prosecution Service but it is possible for one citizen to lay an information related to alleged criminal conduct by another. A well-known provision of the Road Traffic Act allows a defendant in the case of certain minor motoring offences, to escape having to attend court if he pleads "guilty" by post. This useful provision, it must be stressed, does not extend to other cases, in the majority of which the defendant must either be present in person, or be legally represented. In some instances, particularly where there is a possibility of imprisonment, the defendant must attend.

A new statutory provision is for there to be duty solicitors at magistrates' courts available to assist defendants with their defence. The solicitors will be from local firms in private practice and will be paid by the State through the Legal Aid Fund.

When the accused appears before the court for the hearing of the charge, the court will state the substance of the information and ask the accused if he pleads guilty or not guilty. If he pleads guilty, provided he does so unambiguously, he may be convicted and sentenced without more ado; otherwise, a plea of not guilty will be entered, and the prosecutor responsible for the laying of the information will outline the facts. After outlining the facts relating to the case, the prosecutor calls the prosecution witnesses to substantiate those facts; such witnesses are open to examination by both sides. As in all criminal trials in this country, the onus of proof is on the prosecution to prove the case against the person accused. If the magistrates (or in indictable cases, the jury) are left with a reasonable doubt they must acquit the defendant, since he is entitled to the benefit of any doubt. It follows that at the conclusion of the prosecution case the defendant, or his legal representative, may claim that there is no case for him to answer. This submission means, simply, that the evidence produced by the prosecution does not show that the defendant has committed the offence with which he is charged. If the magistrates uphold that submission the case is dismissed forthwith. On the other hand if they do not accept the defence submission that there is no case to answer, the full case for the defence is then presented to the court. Defence witnesses will be called, and the magistrates will finally be left to decide whether or not the evidence is sufficient for them to convict. If they decide to convict they proceed to sentence the defendant; if they decide not to convict the case is dismissed.

The bench of magistrates, from two to seven in number, can call for the assistance of their legally qualified clerk if the case raises issues of law rather than fact. The maximum penalty open to the magistrates, unless a specific statute provides otherwise, is six months' imprisonment, and/or a £2,000 fine. If a defendant is convicted of two or more offences at the same hearing the magistrates have power to send him to prison for 12 months. There is power in the magistrates in many instances to send a convicted defendant for sentence to the next sitting of the Crown Court for that area, if they feel that their own sentencing powers are inadequate. This happens infrequently in that the vast majority of cases can be satisfactorily dealt with by the imposition of a fine.

An appeal in a summary case will take one of two forms. The usual procedure is for the defendant to appeal to the Crown Court, where there is a complete rehearing of the case, including the calling of all the witnesses heard before the magistrates. The decision of the Crown Court is final on the facts of a summary case and there is no further provision for appeal. If, however, the defence raises a point of law in the magistrates' court, or at the Crown Court, then it is possible for an appeal on the point of law to go, by a process known as appeal by way of case stated, for determination to three judges sitting in the Queen's Bench Divisional Court. From the decision of the Divisional Court on the point of law, a further appeal, subject to leave being obtained, is possible to the House of Lords. Such cases are rare; the sort of matter which has gone on appeal to the House of Lords is when technical points, for example relating to the use of breathalyser equipment by the police are raised. The procedure followed in an appeal on a point of law is for the magistrates, through their clerk, to have prepared a statement setting out the point of law raised, and explaining why they ruled on it as they did. This is why the process is known as "a case stated." The Divisional Court or the House of Lords then considers the point of law in question and gives its determination; it restricts itself entirely to the point of law raised and to arguments about it.

Indictable offences

When an individual is charged with a more serious crime—an indictable offence—process may be begun, as with summary offences, by laying an information before a magistrate who will then issue either a summons or a warrant for arrest. But after this the procedure is different. If the person concerned has been arrested, he must be brought before a magistrate within 24 hours (excluding Sunday), so that he may then either be granted bail or remanded in custody. If the magistrates decide to remand him in custody the maximum limit for a remand is eight days. Statutory provisions are contained in the Bail Act 1976.

It is to be noted that the Police and Criminal Evidence Act 1984 contains detailed statutory provisions governing police conduct in relation to arrest and detention, and the questioning and treatment of persons suspected of having committed crime. Depending on circumstances suspects may be detained without charge for up to 96 hours, but this is only likely to occur very exceptionally.

While the accused person is on bail or remand, the prosecution must be actively preparing their case, because the first stage in the procedure is for the magistrates to hold their examination, or preliminary inquiry. This inquiry, which is also known as committal proceedings, is an impartial investigation of the prosecution case. The examining magistrates, usually two in number, hear all the prosecution witnesses and then decide whether or not there is a prima facie case to warrant putting the accused person on trial. It is not at this stage a question of whether the accused is guilty or not guilty, it is a simple test of how substantial is the case against him. Since the onus of proof is on the prosecution, the magistrates can save the time of the court of trial by refusing to commit an accused person where the case against him is too flimsy to warrant a trial. Until recent changes by legislation all the evidence given at these proceedings was taken down in longhand by the clerk of the justices. Each witness had then to swear on oath to the truth of his evidence as contained in this statement, which was called a deposition. This procedure is now known as "old style committal." "New style committal" allows for written statements to be submitted to the examining magistrates if the parties agree; even to the extent of the defendant, if he is legally represented, agreeing that the magistrates may commit him for trial without considering the evidence. In effect this is committal by consent. The main point is that it rests with the defendant how the committal proceedings are to operate. He can, if he wishes, insist on the old style process of oral evidence and depositions; or he can insist on some witnesses giving oral evidence but accept the written evidence of others. The written statement of evidence must be signed; it must contain a declaration, that the person making it believes it to be true and copies must be made available to the defendant. He is thus made fully aware of the case which he will have to meet at the trial. The new committal proceeding arrangements make for much greater speed without restricting the defendant's rights in any way. Another important change has placed a restriction on the press in its publication of committal proceedings. This only permits the publication of the bare details of the names and addresses of the parties, the charges and the decision of the magistrates. An exception is made if the defendant asks for the restrictions on press reporting to be lifted. This change in the law was made on the grounds that as, in committal proceedings, only the prosecution case was published, it could lead to a jury being prejudiced against a defendant. The public can nonetheless attend the committal proceedings.

As might be expected, in the vast majority of cases the examining magistrates are satisfied that the prosecution have a case and so commit the accused person for trial. This invariably means trial by jury at the Crown Court. The actual court is determined by the locality where the alleged criminal act took place and the accused person receives a written statement of the charge—"an indictment." An indictment may be made up of several "counts," or separate charges.

At the Crown Court the accused is arraigned before the court; that is, he is asked whether he pleads "guilty" or "not guilty." If his plea is "guilty" he will be sentenced by the court—the High Court judge, circuit judge or recorder—as soon as the facts have been outlined and his plea in mitigation has been heard. A plea in mitigation is an attempt to stress the factors relevant to the accused and to the crime, which warrant leniency. If the plea is "not guilty" the court proceeds to swear in 12 jurors, who will be responsible at the end of the trial for deciding whether the accused is guilty or not guilty. Once the jury is sworn in, the prosecution will open the case by outlining the facts and then calling the prosecution witnesses to give evidence to prove those facts. The defence can cross-examine all such witnesses. At the close of the prosecution case the defence counsel presents his case and calls witnesses for the defence, possibly including the accused person himself. These witnesses too can be cross-examined on their evidence. It will be noticed that the accused person is not required to give evidence. This rule, sometimes called the right to silence, explains what is meant by saying that the English trial system is "accusatorial" and not "inquisitorial." The court has to decide whether the prosecution's accusation is proved or not, it does not hold an inquiry into the case. If it did do so, it would be forced to have the accused answer questions which were relevant to the circumstances of the alleged crime.

When the final speeches by the prosecution and defence counsel have been made, the judge "sums up" for the benefit of the jury. This is a vital stage because the summing-up is the last speech which the jury hear before they retire to consider their verdict. In it the judge has to balance the arguments of the prosecution and the defence, but leave the jury to decide on the issue of guilt, beyond reasonable doubt, of the accused. Contrary to popular belief the judge must never let the jury know his personal view of the matter.

As a result of another change first introduced by the Criminal Justice Act 1967 it is possible for the judge to accept a majority verdict of the jury provided that there is not more than two in the minority. If there are three or more in the minority there has to be a retrial. If the jury has dropped to 11 or 10 in number there can be a majority verdict if there is not more than one dissenter. However, every effort is made to obtain a unanimous verdict and the jury must have been out for at least two hours before the judge is able to accept a majority verdict. If the jury are unable to agree on their verdict then there will have to be a retrial before another judge and jury. If the verdict is "not guilty" the accused is immediately discharged; if the verdict is "guilty" the accused becomes "the prisoner in the dock" and, after a plea in mitigation by his counsel, he will be sentenced by the judge.

A convicted person may appeal from the Crown Court to the Criminal Division of the Court of Appeal. He must give notice of doing so within 28 days of conviction or sentence. He may appeal against *conviction* on a point of law as of right, but to appeal against conviction on a point of fact or of mixed law and fact he must have the leave of either the trial judge or the Court of Appeal. The Court of Appeal may also give him leave to appeal on "any other grounds which appears to the Court of Appeal to be a sufficient ground of appeal." If he appeals against *sentence* he will always require the leave of the Court of Appeal and there are other restrictions upon his right of appeal. Where the leave of the Court of Appeal is required, applications for leave may be, and normally are, dealt with by a single judge in private without any legal representatives being present. If the application is refused by the single judge, the applicant is entitled to have his application dealt with by the Court of Appeal, which customarily consists of two judges who always hear the application orally and in public.

It should be noted that the court may review the sentence in a case, but it is unlikely lightly to set aside the verdict of the jury. In theory a further appeal to the House of Lords is possible by the prosecution or the defence, but only if the Court of Appeal certifies that the case reveals a point of law of general public importance and either that court or the House of Lords grants leave on the principle that the point is one which ought to be considered by the House of Lords (see further Chapter 6, above, p. 63). An occasional criminal appeal does reach the House of Lords but there are only, on average nine each year. Often an appeal will be concerned with "technical" law in such fields as the admissibility of evidence.

Offences triable either way

The Criminal Law Act 1977 stipulated three modes of trial based on three categories of offence. First, offences triable only on indictment. These are offences which are not the subject of an express statutory provision affecting the other two categories. Second, offences triable only summarily. These are offences which Parliament has specifically designated as triable summarily. Third, offences triable either way. These offences were specified in a substantial list in schedule 3 of the Act. The list included most charges of theft and assault and criminal damage over £200.

The Magistrates Courts Act 1980 lays down that for an offence triable either way the magistrates' court shall hear representations from the prosecutor and the defendant as to the appropriate mode of trial. (The court has no discretion if the Attorney General or the Director of Public Prosecutions seeks indictable trial). Having heard the representations and considered all the circumstances the magistrates may decide that the defendant should be tried on indictment. If so, that decision is final. If they consider that summary trial is appropriate the magistrates tell the defendant so, but they must inform him that he can either agree to summary trial or insist on trial by jury. Experience has shown that the vast majority of defendants who have an option choose to have the case tried by magistrates.

4. Royal Commission on Criminal Procedure

A Royal Commission on Criminal Procedure reported in 1981 and many of its recommendations have been enacted. The Criminal Justice Act 1982 made changes in the sentencing powers pertaining to the criminal courts; the Prosecution of Offences Act 1985 instituted a Crown Prosecution Service in place of prosecution by the police; and the Police and Criminal Evidence Act 1984 introduced a comprehensive code of police powers and practices in the investigation of crime and amended the rules of evidence in criminal proceedings in certain respects.

5. Sentences

As a postscript to this chapter on procedure in criminal cases, a short consideration of the punishment which can be ordered by the courts is necessary. Most of the law on this subject is now to be found in the Powers of Criminal Courts Act 1973 and the Criminal Justice Act 1982.

The general principle is that the sentence of the court lies in the discretion of the judge, subject only to the maximum limits imposed by Parliament; but, as might be expected, an effort is made to ensure that there is consistency in the treatment of offenders, linked with the need for full weight to be given to the individual circumstances of the defendant.

Death

The death penalty has been abolished for murder, but it theoretically remains possible in cases of treason and piracy.

Imprisonment

The punishment for murder, and the maximum punishment for manslaughter, is life imprisonment. In the case of a life sentence for murder the judge may stipulate the minimum period which should elapse before the defendant is released on licence. In most other cases Parliament has fixed an upper limit and the courts exercise their discretion in deciding the actual term of imprisonment to apply to the individual case.

One possibility is that a sentence of imprisonment may be imposed but suspended. This can only be so where the term of imprisonment is two years or less. The sentence is suspended for from one to two years and only takes effect if the person concerned is convicted of an offence punishable by imprisonment within that period of time, and the court so decides. A person under 21 cannot be sentenced to imprisonment.

Fine

The main alternative to imprisonment is for the court to impose a money penalty, payable to the state, and known as a fine. A term of imprisonment is sometimes specified as an alternative to the payment of the fine. As has been seen magistrates are limited to a £2,000 maximum fine and in order to secure payment, a court can now use the attachment of earnings procedure.

Youth custody sentence

A youth custody order is used for young men and women aged between 15 and 21 where the sentence imposed is four months or more. A sentence of custody for life is possible in similar circumstances to an adult being sentenced to life imprisonment. The law on custody and detention of offenders under the age of 21 is to be found in the Criminal Justice Act 1982. Normally supervision will follow release from youth custody.

Detention centre orders

A detention centre order is used for male persons aged 14 to 21 where the sentence is for a period of between 21 days and four months. Supervision will follow release.

Attendance centre orders

An attendance centre order may be made for a person under 21, who could otherwise be sentenced to youth custody or a detention centre. Attendance will normally be for 12 hours, but can be for 24 or 36 hours depending on age.

Probation

A probation order can be made for an offender age 17 or over provided he is willing to be bound by the order. Probation lasts from six months to three years and takes the place of punishment. Conditions may be imposed such as a requirement as to residence, or as to attendance at a day training centre. If there is a breach of the conditions in the order the person concerned can be sentenced for the original offence.

Binding over

This order requires the offender to enter into recognisances to be of good behaviour, and possibly attaches other conditions. It applies usually in lieu of sentence.

Absolute and conditional discharge

If a court decides that no punishment for an offence is called for, it may discharge the person concerned either absolutely, in which case that is the end of the matter, or conditionally, in which case the offender must not commit another offence for from one to three years as specified. If he does, he can be sentenced for the original offence.

Mental Health Order

Where a person is convicted of an offence punishable by imprisonment, the court can make a hospital order or a guardianship order, which requires the detention of the offender in a suitable hospital.

Compensation or Criminal Bankruptcy Order

A court may order an offender convicted of an indictable offence to pay a sum by way of compensation to the party who has suffered loss as a result of his criminal conduct. Where the criminal conduct has involved a loss of £15,000 or more the court may, in addition to any other punishment, make a criminal bankruptcy order.

Restitution

Following a conviction for theft a court can order the restitution of the actual goods to the owner of them. If the goods have been sold, the court can order the transfer of any other goods bought by the thief with the proceeds of the sale to the owner. It can also order the payment of the value of the goods to be made to the owner out of money found in the possession of the person convicted.

Community Service Order

This order, which must have the consent of the convicted person, can apply to persons over the age of 16, but only, at present, in certain areas. The person agrees to work unpaid for between 40 and 240 hours as ordered in the interests of the community. If he fails to observe the terms of the order he can be fined up to £50 and sentenced for the original offence.

Remission of sentence and parole

Normally, a person sentenced to imprisonment can obtain remission of one-third of the sentence imposed. Remission may be forfeited for misconduct whilst serving the prison sentence.

Parliament has established a Parole Board to operate a system under which a person imprisoned for 18 months or more can be released on parole after serving one-third of his sentence subject to undergoing a minimum of 6 months' imprisonment. The release is on licence and is subject to supervision. The scheme does not apply to life sentences.

Compensation and costs on acquittal

Although there is as yet no statutory scheme to compensate persons acquitted in criminal trials, nor even for persons wrongly convicted, there are provisions, the latest in the Prosecution of Offences Act 1985, under which the costs of a successful defendant may be ordered to be met out of central funds.

Forfeiture

Under the Drug Trafficking Offences Act 1986 the assets resulting from criminal activity may be seized by the Crown. Proposed legislation would extend this power to gains accruing from other crimes.

The Criminal Injuries Compensation Board

Established in 1964, the Criminal Injuries Compensation Board was brought into being under the royal prerogative to deal with applications for compensation from the victims of violent crime. The board is made up of a chairman and eight members, all of whom are legally qualified. Its function is to hold informal private hearings and make *ex gratia* payments to persons whose claims are approved. The basis of assessment is the comparable compensation approach of common law damages and the total amount distributed annually is now running at approximately 35 million. Details of the more important claims submitted, and the payments made, are published regularly.

Under proposed legislation the Board would become a statutory body. In recent years it has been nearly overwhelmed with new claims.

8. Evidence

1. Meaning

Chapter 7 has dealt with the standard procedure which is followed in both a civil and a criminal case, and it is now necessary to consider, in outline, the law of evidence as it applies to such cases.

Because the courts will not deal with hypothetical circumstances, every court case is concerned with disputes arising from actual facts. The task of the court is to unravel and identify the relevant facts in the case, and then determine the dispute for the parties by applying the appropriate legal principles to those facts. The law of evidence assists the court to this objective by establishing rules about the means by which the facts of a case are to be presented to the court. The facts which are at the basis of the dispute between the parties, whether in a civil or a criminal case, are called "the facts in issue"; and in every case it will be the substantive law and procedure which will decide which facts are the facts in issue. Evidence comes into its own in that it is the branch of the law which provides the means by which those facts in issue can be proved.

Some of the confusion associated with the law of evidence arises because there are at least three senses in which the word can be used.

   (i) In the formal legal sense, as described above, the word is used to mean the way in which the facts in issue can be proved.

  (ii) By a natural abbreviation the word is sometimes used to describe those facts which may be proved, instead of the means by which those facts may be proved.

 (iii) The word is frequently used alone in the sense of "admissible evidence," where the consideration is whether or not the facts in question are, under the principles of the law of evidence, such as the court will permit to be given in the manner proposed or not. In such instances the evidence is said to be "admissible," or "inadmissible," as the rules allow.

It will be gathered that the law of evidence is not an easy subject, and it has been vigorously criticised as by C. P. Harvey, Q.C., in his book, *The Advocate's Devil*, where he writes: "Founded apparently on the propositions that all jurymen are deaf to reason, that all witnesses are presumptively liars, and that all documents are presumptively forgeries, it has been added to, subtracted from and tinkered with, until it has become less of a structure than a pile of builder's debris." Nevertheless, the experience of other legal systems has shown that there is a need for a law of evidence, and the pages which follow will endeavour to select some of the more important aspects of the subject for consideration. What is certain is that it is impossible to understand the method of trial in a civil or criminal case without an appreciation of the relevant rules of procedure and evidence.

2. The Burden of Proof

The fundamental factor in any legal case is the burden of proof.

In a civil case the courts take the view that the responsibility for proving the facts alleged to substantiate the claim made, or the defence submitted, falls on the party propounding those facts. It can thus be said that the general burden of proof is fixed at the beginning of the trial on the plaintiff, or the defendant, asserting the affirmative of an issue. Once that evidence has been given, however, the particular burden of proof may shift throughout the trial as each party gives in turn his version of the facts in dispute.

In a criminal case, because the English system follows the accusatorial principle whereby the prosecution accuses the defendant of committing a specified criminal offence, the onus of proving that the defendant is guilty of the offence charged is entirely on the prosecution. The prosecution cannot look to the defendant for any assistance in the case, in that he cannot be required to answer questions or afford explanations of his conduct. If he wishes, the defendant can remain silent throughout the proceedings. This means that the prosecution in bringing a case must have sufficient evidence available to satisfy the court, "beyond reasonable doubt," that the accused person is guilty of the offence with which he is charged.

The direct result of this approach is the long accepted principle of the criminal law that the defendant is entitled to be presumed innocent until the prosecution have satisfied the court that he is guilty beyond reasonable doubt. There are, exceptionally, a limited number of situations in which the defendant in a criminal case may have the burden of proving particular facts. For example, if the defence sets up a plea of insanity or diminished responsibility, it is for the defence to satisfy the court that this plea is justified. Again under section 25 of the Theft Act 1968 where a person is found in possession of any article for use in the course of, or in connection with, any burglary, theft or cheat, it may well fall to the defendant to justify his possession of the article.

Finally, having disposed of "the burden," the further question arises, what is "proof"? The *Oxford English Dictionary"* defines "proof" as the process which convinces the mind of something and in the evidential sense this occurs when the court accepts that a particular circumstance has been shown to its satisfaction to be a relevant fact in issue.

One vital difference between civil and criminal cases in this matter of the burden of proof is that whereas in a civil case the court will work on the preponderance of probability, in a criminal case, because the freedom of the individual may be involved, a higher standard is applied and the proof is required to be beyond reasonable doubt.

3. Types of Evidence

(i) Oral evidence

The word "evidence" comes from the Latin word "videre," meaning "to see," so that oral evidence is the testimony of a witness given by word of mouth relating to a matter which he has actually seen or of which he has some direct personal knowledge. In giving his testimony on oath in public as a witness, the person called before the court is subjected to an examination in three stages. He is first asked to answer certain questions by the party who is calling him. This is known as examination-in-chief. Then when this is concluded the legal representative of the other party will proceed to ask the witness questions, designed to show that his testimony is not reliable, or to get him to admit to facts which correspond to the other party's side of the case. This stage is known as cross-examination. Finally the side which originally called the witness is allowed to clarify, by further questions, the answers given by the witness in cross-examination. No new material can be introduced. This stage is known as re-examination.

(ii) Documentary evidence

In many civil cases much of the evidence before the court will consist of relevant documents as, for example, the correspondence which has passed between the parties, or the various contract documents relating to the claim. Similarly in certain criminal cases, such as fraud or forgery, a document or documents can be relevant evidence.

The court will usually require to see and inspect the original document, and in civil procedure there is provision for what is called Discovery of Documents, so that the parties and the court have access to all relevant documents in advance of the hearing.

If an original document is not available the court may be prepared to accept a carbon copy, or even evidence of the contents of a missing document, for example, a will, depending on the circumstances.

(iii) Real evidence

Real evidence usually takes the form of the inspection of a material object by the court. The poker alleged to have been the murder weapon, or the second-hand car the subject of the contract, may be examined by the court as a means of proof of a relevant fact in issue. Such objects are usually called "exhibits."

If it is not convenient to bring an object into court, or if the court wishes to inspect a building, or make a site visit, then this "view" is taken to be real evidence. The same term is used of the impression which a witness makes on the court resulting from his demeanour in the witness-box.

4. Classification of Evidence

(i) Direct evidence and circumstantial evidence

Direct evidence relates to the facts in issue themselves. For example, the witness, who actually saw the incident which gives rise to the criminal charge, or which is a vital aspect of a civil case, can give direct evidence. Similarly an original document or a material object which is, in itself, a fact in issue is direct evidence.

Circumstantial evidence is evidence of certain facts from which the facts in issue can be inferred. The presentation to the court of a number of related circumstances—or facts not in issue—can lead to the inference in a criminal case that the accused is guilty of the crime charged. A murder case, where the body of the victim has not been found, is a clear instance of a situation where circumstantial evidence is likely to be the only evidence available to prove the charge. Inevitably with circumstantial evidence, the arguments will be about the proper inferences to be drawn from the evidence.

(ii) Primary and secondary evidence

Primary evidence is the most effective evidence to prove a particular fact in issue. The witness who saw the incident is to be preferred to a person who heard his version some time later; the actual letter, containing an alleged offer in a contract case, is to be preferred to the recollection of one of the parties as to the terms of the letter.

Secondary evidence is the term used to describe evidence which is introduced to take the place of certain primary evidence which is not available to the court. In the case of a document this may be a copy of the original or other evidence relating to its contents.

At one time the courts had a rule that only the "best evidence" of the facts in issue would be allowed. This rule has been relaxed, so that now the courts will permit the facts to be proved by any admissible means. Obviously, however, the courts will expect the parties to call primary rather than secondary evidence, unless good reason for the failure can be shown.

(iii) Original and hearsay evidence

The difference between these two kinds of evidence is, in general terms, the difference between first-hand evidence and second-hand evidence.

Original evidence may be oral, documentary or real as, for example, the witness who was present at the incident, in question and can testify of his own knowledge as to what took place.

Hearsay evidence, in contrast, is evidence of what some other person, who is not before the court, has said or written. Naturally the attitude of the courts is to insist, in so far as this is possible, that that other person should himself or herself be brought before the court, so that the court can itself assess the demeanour of the witness, and the opposing party can proceed to cross-examine him or her on what he or she has said or written. For this reason the courts have been unwilling to accept hearsay evidence where it is presented as proof of the truth of what was said or written. Confusion can arise because what appears to be hearsay may in another sense be properly treated as original evidence; for example, if it is presented to the court to prove that a statement was made or a letter was written.

In criminal cases the general principle is that hearsay evidence is inadmissible. This rule has been relaxed to allow certain declarations of deceased persons to be put in as evidence, as also voluntary confessions by the accused and certain statements contained in public documents. The rule has been further relaxed by statute, the most recent example being the Police and Criminal Evidence Act 1984 which permits a document forming part of a record of a trade or business to be admitted as evidence of a matter so recorded. The

Act also covers records in the public sector as well as allowing computer records and microfilm entries to be admissible subject to various conditions.

In civil cases the rule against hearsay has been substantially relaxed by statute and is consequently much less important. Whereas confessions in a criminal case are the subject of detailed law to prevent oppression and can only be made by the accused, in a civil case an admission need not be made voluntarily and may be made by agent, counsel or solicitor. This explains why letters relating to the possible compromise of a claim in a civil case are headed with the words "without prejudice" since the letter cannot then be given in evidence. If the position were otherwise, the letter containing the offer to settle might be taken to be an admission of liability.

The Civil Evidence Act 1968, which was substantially the brain child of the Law Reform Committee (see p. 183), resulted from the recommendations in its thirteenth report published in 1966 and called *Hearsay Evidence in Civil Proceedings.* The Act goes most of the way towards abolishing the hearsay rule in civil proceedings, thus taking a stage further the inroads into the rule made by the Evidence Act 1938, which it largely repeals. The 1968 Act implements the main recommendation of the report which was expressed in this way: "All statements, whether written or oral, which tended to establish a fact of which direct oral evidence would be admissible would themselves be potentially admissible if proved to have been made by a person who had, or might reasonably be supposed to have, personal knowledge of the matters dealt with in the statement. So would written or mechanically recorded statements made by any person in performance of a duty to record information supplied to him by a person who either himself had personal knowledge of the facts so recorded, or was under a duty to transmit such information, where the information transmitted originated from a person who had such personal knowledge." It was felt that by appropriate rules of procedure the parties in a civil matter could be protected against any conceivable abuse by the introduction of hearsay evidence. Such rules have since been made.

Another provision of the Act lays down that the findings of a court in a criminal case are to be available as evidence in any subsequent civil case. This provision will, *inter alia*, prevent the virtual reopening of the criminal case in the hope of getting a change of verdict, by the commencement of civil proceedings, for example, defamation, based on the same facts.

It remains the position that hearsay evidence which has no relevance to the facts in issue, whether in civil or criminal cases, is, like other forms of evidence which are irrelevant, inadmissible.

5. Differences in the Law of Evidence in Civil and Criminal Cases

General

Although the principles of the law of evidence are common to both civil and criminal cases, certain special rules apply in criminal cases. One such difference was observed in the treatment of the hearsay rule where the criminal case approach is much more stringent. Other examples are:

(i) Waiver. Evidence can, at the discretion of the parties, be waived in civil but not in criminal cases. This distinction follows the fundamental rule that a civil action can be "settled out of court" by the parties before trial and can be settled with the approval of the court during the trial, whereas criminal proceedings, once begun, cannot be withdrawn unless the court gives its consent.

(ii) Character. The rules relating to the giving of evidence of character differ as between civil and criminal cases.

In a civil case the plaintiff may not give evidence of his own good character nor call a witness to give such evidence. On the other hand a witness can be cross-examined as to his character so as to test his credit as to the evidence he has given. In the occasional case, as, for example, where justification is pleaded as a defence in defamation, the character of the plaintiff may be a relevant factor in which case evidence of his character may be given.

In a criminal case the prosecution must not buttress its case by deducing evidence of the accused's bad character to support its allegations against him. If, however, the accused himself puts his character in evidence, or if he attacks the character of the prosecution witnesses, then in either case the prosecution can cross-examine him as to his character and bring any previous convictions of the accused to light except where these are to be treated as "spent" in accordance with the Rehabilitation of Offenders Act 1974 (see p. 90 below).

(iii) Admissions. In a civil case, as was seen in the chapter on procedure, the documents which make up the pleadings must expressly answer every allegation contained in the opponent's claim. Any such allegation, which is not expressly denied, or traversed, is taken to be admitted.

By way of contrast in a criminal case the prosecution has to prove every factor relevant to the guilt of the accused. The only qualification to this rule is that, it is permissible for the defence to make formal admissions to the court in order to obviate the need for those particular facts to be specifically proved.

(iv) Confessions. Whereas confessions are inapplicable in civil proceedings, they are of vital importance in a criminal case.

The Police and Criminal Evidence Act 1984 has replaced the former Judges' Rules with statutory provisions designed to exclude confessions obtained by oppression or in any circumstances which might render the confession unreliable. There are also provisions under which evidence obtained unfairly can be excluded by the court.

(v) Previous convictions. A fundamental rule in criminal trials is that the court must not be told of the previous convictions (if any) of the defendant

Save in the exceptional circumstances specified, the Rehabilitation of Offenders Act 1974 provides that after certain periods of time a conviction is to be regarded as "spent." The length of time in question varies with the sentence imposed. Sentences of more than 30 months' imprisonment are excluded from rehabilitation. Once a conviction is "spent" it must no longer be referred to. Subject to this legislation the court is formally informed of the previous convictions of the defendant after he has been found "guilty" and is about to be sentenced.

(vi) Complaints and corroboration. In a number of criminal cases, most of them involving sexual offences, special rules of evidence apply—(a) relating to the conduct of the victim in making a complaint at the first opportunity, and (b) requiring the evidence given by the one party to be corroborated by other evidence relevant to the matter.

(vii) Identification evidence. The problem of visual identification evidence constantly gives cause for concern. Every year there seems to be at least one case, and sometimes several, where a conviction is set aside because the innocence of the person convicted has been established. On investigation it becomes clear that the conviction was obtained through witnesses who visually, but mistakenly, identified the defendant.

In *R.* v. *Turnbull* (1976) the Lord Chief Justice sitting with a full court in the Court of Appeal (Criminal Division) gave detailed advice to judges presiding in cases where visual identification evidence is all important.

(viii) Alibi as a defence. An important statutory provision requires the defence in a criminal case to give the prosecution notice of its intention to rely on an alibi at the pending trial. Full details of the alibi must be given at the committal proceedings or within seven days thereafter. This precludes an alibi of dubious authenticity being sprung on the prosecution at the trial.

(ix) Opinions. The general principle is that the opinions of witnesses are not relevant, because the court in every case is concerned with the proof of facts. The one exception made is that the opinion of an expert witness, for example a doctor, may be accepted where the opinion is based directly on his expert knowledge.

(x) Estoppel. This rule of evidence prevents a party, usually in a civil action, from asserting or denying a particular fact. For example, once a decision in a matter has been arrived at by a court, that matter is said to be *"res judicata,"* and that issue cannot be raised again. Where it applies estoppel results in a party being "stopped" from introducing evidence, which would otherwise be admissible. Estoppel may arise by agreement, by representation, by conduct or by deed.

(xi) Judicial notice. One qualification to the rule that all relevant facts must be proved is that in civil and criminal cases the judge will take notice of such matters as the contents of Acts of Parliament or the law and custom of Parliament. Facts of which judicial notice is taken do not therefore require to be proved.

(xii) Compelling attendance. A court has long reserved the power to compel a witness to attend and give evidence before it. In civil proceedings the court may issue a document, called a subpoena, which will require the attendance of a witness; in criminal proceedings the Criminal Procedure (Attendance of Witnesses) Act 1965 allows for the making of a witness order, or witness summons, to compel attendance. A failure to attend then becomes a contempt of court.

There are a few exceptions where a person will not be made to be a witness, for example a wife, or husband, is not normally compelled to give evidence in criminal proceedings against the other spouse. Another example of a very different kind is that, in civil and criminal proceedings, persons enjoying diplomatic immunity cannot be compelled to give evidence.

(xiii) Public policy. In a criminal case it is a matter of public policy whether or not a prosecution is proceeded with, and the Crown by a writ of *nolle prosequi* can always intervene to terminate proceedings in progress.

In a civil case the courts have long accepted that, as a matter of public policy, the Crown has the right to decline to allow apparently relevant evidence to be given. This is known as Crown Privilege or privilege in the public interest. Obviously the claim is not to be lightly accepted by the courts, and in *Conway* v. *Rimmer* (1968) the House of Lords laid down that, in every such instance, the court will require the central government Minister concerned to justify the claim that it is not in the public interest for the evidence to be given.

9. Tribunals, Inquiries and Arbitration

1. Tribunals

Function

In addition to the civil and criminal courts, which have been examined in Chapters 5 and 6, there also exists in the English legal system a vast number of tribunals set up by Acts of Parliament to hear and decide disputes on a court-like basis. These tribunals are frequently referred to as "administrative tribunals," because many of the issues which arise and need to be determined do so under a statutory scheme of administration. Examples are the Social Security Tribunals which were originally set up under the National Insurance Act 1946 to hear claims to unemployment, sickness and death benefits and to old age and widows' pensions. It was plainly foreseeable that, when the national insurance system was brought into operation by the Act, there would be disputed decisions and so provision was made for the establishment of these administrative tribunals. Thus in some instances the conflict is between the citizen on the one side and a state agency on the other, but this is not always the case; there have been examples of Parliament setting up tribunals where the dispute is between two individuals. Perhaps the best example in this field is the creation of rent tribunals charged with the task of fixing a reasonable rent for the letting of certain furnished or unfurnished properties. Although no state agency is involved, the whole question of housing is of vital interest to the government, and the landlord and tenant relationship, in consequence, has been the subject of controls for many years.

There is complete diversity of function amongst administrative tribunals and no classification is completely satisfactory. There are tribunals concerned with the various social services' legislation covering claims for industrial injuries, supplementary benefits, service pensions and redundancy payments, and tribunals reviewing the detention of persons mentally afflicted and hearing complaints about the professional conduct of doctors under the National Health Service scheme. There are tribunals concerned with matters affecting agricultural land, public transport, the valuation of land, income tax assessments and a wide range of more specialised matters extending from copyright in plant varieties, to betting levy assessments and immigration appeals. All that can be said is that in every instance Parliament has brought the tribunal into being and given it limited jurisdiction over the matters specified in the Act.

There is no reason why the dispute in question should not have been given to a court to decide, and in this sense the use of tribunals is best seen as an extension of, or supplement to, the court system. It is not a worthwhile exercise to try to distinguish a court from a tribunal, since to a spectator their appearance is one and the same. Both are bodies responsible for determining disputes.

Advantages and disadvantages

The reasons which are advanced for the use of tribunals rather than the ordinary court are several. A major consideration is that the costs of a tribunal hearing are negligible, particularly as compared with a High Court action. There are no court fees to the parties and as legal representation is not essential the costs of this can be avoided. Tribunals can give a fixed date for the hearing in contrast to court proceedings where the case is entered in the list and all parties and witnesses have to be present to await the case being called, which inevitably increases the cost of an action brought in the courts.

In order to put the parties at their ease and to obviate the need for legal representation the procedure followed at a tribunal hearing is as informal as possible. There is nothing like the formal rules of court or the documentary method of proceeding—the pleadings— used in the High Court. The members of the tribunal can take part in the proceedings and may assist either or both parties in the presentation of the case. Hearings are held to suit the convenience of the parties and as far as possible tribunals are accessible in that they sit locally and as business demands. At the conclusion of the hearing the tribunal arrives at its decision, which may be announced forthwith or notified to the parties reasonably quickly after the hearing.

Another important factor in favour of tribunals is that the members of a tribunal, because of their limited jurisdiction, soon become specialists in the particular field of law with which they are concerned. The members of a Rent Tribunal inevitably become expert on the level of rents within their locality; and similar expertise is a

chracteristic of all tribunal work. Whereas a judge has a wide jurisdiction, a tribunal member rapidly becomes a specialist; this leads to
a consistency of treatment of cases locally which cannot be matched
by the courts. The system also has the advantage of bringing laymen
into the legal system, as with magistrates and jurors, so ensuring
that the lawyers are not the totally dominant force in all disputes. In
fact the composition of a tribunal, as will be seen, is almost always a
combination of lawyer and laymen.

Perhaps the most important argument in favour of the system is
that if all the tribunals were abolished the courts would simply be
unable to cope with the work which would have to be transferred to
them. It has been estimated that tribunals deal in total with
approximately one quarter of a million cases every year. The Benson
Report highlighted this matter (paragraph 15.1) by pointing out
that "the total number of cases heard by tribunals in 1978 was six
times the number of contested civil cases that were disposed of at
trial before the High Court and county courts. The number of hearing days in tribunals has in recent years exceeded the total number
of hearing days before judges in the High Court and county court,
including days in chambers."

Those persons who can see disadvantages in the tribunal system
point to the dangers of having a cheap, informal hearing with an
immediate decision; they point out that the rules of court, the pleadings, and the formal procedure and rules of evidence of the courts
are there because experience has shown that these lead in the long
run to the most satisfactory result—the establishment of legal principles in accordance with the ideals of justice. They regard this by-
passing of the court system as a dangerous lowering of standards,
and foresee the introduction of tribunals by the executive as a matter
of administrative expediency, whenever new legislation calls for the
resolving of disputes.

Judging from the continuing use made of tribunals by successive
governments and their willingness to establish new tribunals, the
critics are not making much headway.

Characteristics
Creation
All tribunals are of statutory origin and share one common
feature, the task of adjudication.

Composition
The composition of an administrative tribunal varies from one to
another. Whereas a Lands Tribunal hearing consists of one member

to decide the dispute, an Industrial Tribunal hearing will require three members to be present. In general terms the majority of tribunals will be made up of three members, with a lawyer chairman and two lay representatives. For Social Security Tribunals and the Industrial Tribunals the lay representatives will be selected from nominations made by employers and union organisations, and for Agricultural Land Tribunals the two lay representatives are in the same way chosen from nominations of the County Landowners' Association and the National Farmers' Union. Where the tribunal is concerned with specialist matters, as in the case of the Medical Appeal Tribunal, which assesses the degree of medical disability from which a claimant is suffering, inevitably the tribunal is made up of experts, in this instance medical specialists of consultant status.

The appointment of members to serve on tribunals usually falls, under the statute creating the tribunal, to the minister of the central government department whose ministry is responsible for the service to which the tribunal's jurisdiction relates. Accordingly the Secretary of State for the Environment appoints members of Rent Tribunals and the Secretary of State for the Social Services appoints members of the Supplementary Benefits Appeal Tribunals. The minister is usually guided by the nominations of interested organisations, but he retains a discretion in the matter. In appointing a lawyer chairman, however, the minister is usually required by section 7 of the Tribunals and Inquiries Act 1971 to select from a panel of names of lawyers maintained by the Lord Chancellor.

Members of tribunals are appointed for a limited term, and the minister can then choose whether or not to re-appoint the members at the expiry of their term of office. If a minister wishes to dismiss a member during his term of office, he has to obtain the consent of the Lord Chancellor or of certain other senior judges to the dismissal. This requirement is contained in section 8 of the Tribunals and Inquiries Act 1971.

Procedure

Although there are procedural rules affecting certain tribunals for example, the Mental Health Review Tribunal Rules 1983, made as a statutory instrument under the authority of the Mental Health Act 1983, other tribunals have no formal rules of procedure. Nonetheless all tribunals tend to follow a similar pattern, since they are all determining disputes and consequently all have a court-like appearance. However, at the hearing, as has been seen, informality predominates. Where there are rules they deal with such matters as the composition of the tribunal, the time and place of the hearing, the right of audience and representation, the hearing and the procedure to be adopted, inspection (if applicable) and the notification of the tribunal's decision to the parties.

Cases

The appendix to the annual report of the Council on Tribunals indicates the case-load for that year of all the tribunals supervised by that body.

In all years the General and Special Commissioners of Income Tax and the Social Security Appeal Tribunals consistently head the list. In each of these jurisdictions the total of cases dealt with approaches 100,000.

Even allowing that such case-loads are exceptional the statistics for 1984/85 do emphasise the diversity which characterises the tribunal system. The Local Valuation Courts dealt with 40,000 rate assessment disputes, Rent Assessment Committees heard 16,000 cases, Industrial Tribunals 13,000, Medical Appeal Tribunals 12,500, Traffic Commissioners 10,000, Dairy Produce Quotas Tribunals 10,000 and Immigration Appeals 8,500.

Tribunals with smaller case-loads include the Mental Health Tribunal 2,000, the National Health Service Tribunal 1,500, the Value Added Tax Tribunal 750, the Lands Tribunal 700, and the Agricultural Lands Tribunal 350.

Those tribunals with very small case-loads are the Vaccine Damage Payments Tribunal 38, the Betting Levy Appeal Tribunal 36, the Misuse of Drugs Tribunal 3, the Plant Varieties and Seeds Tribunal 2 and the Performing Rights Tribunal 1.

Organisation of tribunals

The organisation of tribunals depends entirely on the statute which creates the tribunals.

The tribunals concerned with Social Security problems are, as might be expected, organised on a national basis.

For rating assessment disputes there are 64 panels in England and Wales, whereas for mental health orders reviewed by tribunals there are 15 tribunals; the same number of regional offices supervise the Industrial Tribunals, whilst there are 13 regional Rent Assessment Committees. There are eight Agricultural Land Tribunals, two Value Added Tax tribunals but only one Transport Tribunal and one Performing Right Tribunal. The latter sit only in London, whilst in contrast the Lands Tribunal holds its sittings wherever business demands.

Appeal

Because generally tribunals are intended to decide issues involving fact, there is no appeal from most tribunals on the facts. One exception is the Social Security Commissioners, qualified barristers, who hear appeals from the determinations of the Social Security Tribunals; another is the Lands Tribunal which hears appeals from Local Valuation courts.

Appeal on a point of law is possible to the High Court under section 13 of the Tribunals and Inquiries Act 1971, which gives that right to any person appearing before any of the tribunals listed in that Act. If a tribunal misconducts itself, or makes a mistake of law, an interested party can call on the Queen's Bench Divisional Court to intervene. This court has powers to control all inferior courts and tribunals, if they make a mistake of law.

The term "tribunal"

As well as the administrative tribunal, the word is also familiar in the term, "domestic tribunal." Such a tribunal is one concerned with the discipline of members of a particular profession or organisation. Solicitors, for example, are subject to the disciplinary code enforced by the Disciplinary Tribunal of the Law Society; the same sort of disciplinary institution is used by doctors, architects and surveyors, and has become common under trade unions' rules. There is the possibility of appeal to the courts against the findings of certain domestic tribunals, *e.g.* to the Privy Council from the General Medical Council.

Another tribunal, which in practice takes the form of an inquiry, is that established by Parliament under the Tribunals of Inquiry (Evidence) Act 1921 to investigate a matter of "urgent public importance." The Aberfan Tribunal was a case in point. A Royal Commission on Tribunals of Inquiry with Lord Salmon as chairman has recommended that Parliament should use this power sparingly. With all the publicity that such a tribunal of inquiry attracts, there is a danger that individuals involved will get less protection than they would have had in an action in a court of law.

The development of the administrative tribunal system

Administrative tribunals, as an important feature of the legal system, are of comparatively recent origin, having achieved particular prominence in the last 40 years. This is not to say that there were no tribunals in earlier years, but the use of tribunals developed rapidly with the advent of the Labour Government in 1945, committed, as it was, to the introduction of "the welfare state." As each statute became law so it was necessary to have a tribunal to deal with the disputes which would arise. The National Insurance and Industrial Injuries Tribunals, the Supplementary Benefits Appeal Tribunal (then the National Assistance Appeals Tribunal), the National Health Service Tribunal and the Medical Appeal Tribunal were all established at this time.

The success of the tribunal both as a body for determining disputes, and for regulating functions, is evidenced by the willingness of the government, through Parliament, to create new tribunals. The Dairy Produce Quota Tribunal, the Data Protection Tribunal and the Residential Homes Tribunal, for example, were all set up under 1984 legislation.

Naturally the increasing use of tribunals has been called in question from time to time. The Committee on Ministers' Powers, which reported in 1932 (the Donoughmore Committee Report, 1932, Cmnd. 4060), was more concerned with delegated legislation, but it considered the place of tribunals in administrative jurisdiction generally. Then the Franks Committee on Administrative Tribunals and Enquiries, which reported in 1957 (the Franks Report, 1957, Cmnd. 218), carried out a thorough examination into the whole system of tribunals and inquiries. Its report remains a book of reference for all those interested in the subject.

The Committee's Report was reassuring about the need for tribunals and inquiries in modern government and about the standards achieved. The Committee, basing its recommendations on the need for "openness, fairness and impartiality," contented itself with seeking to improve the system. Its many proposals were promptly given effect by administrative changes and by legislation.

The latter, as well as setting up the Council on Tribunals, has ensured that tribunals must give reasons for their decisions, that on points of law there should be an appeal to the High Court, that chairmen of most tribunals should be drawn from a panel of lawyers, that the dismissal of members of tribunals should need the consent of the Lord Chancellor and that wherever possible rules of procedure should be prepared, approved and published for tribunals and inquiries.

The Council on Tribunals

The most important recommendation of the Franks Committee was that there should be a standing body responsible for the supervision of tribunals and inquiries. This was given effect immediately by legislation which established the Council on Tribunals. The Council consists of from 10 to 15 part-time lay members and has to report annually to Parliament on the operation of tribunals and inquiries. If the Council wishes it can submit a special report to Parliament at any time. It investigates complaints from members of the public, instigates its own examination of the way in which the system is working and assists the central government departments which are responsible for the membership of tribunals and for the procedural rules under which tribunals and inquiries are held.

2. Inquiries

Function

Although inquiries have in name come to be associated with tribunals, they are designed to serve a quite different purpose. Whereas tribunals, like courts, are intended to reach a decision, inquiries are set up to obtain facts and opinions from all the parties concerned on the matter in issue so that the person, who has to make the decision following on the inquiry, can do so from a fully informed standpoint. Generally an administrative inquiry is held to provide a minister with the fullest possible information before he comes to a policy decision. Such an inquiry has a secondary value in that it enables interested parties to feel that their views have been fully aired and made known to the person making the decision. How far such a process is to be regarded as "letting off steam," and exactly what effect it has on the policy-makers, is something which cannot easily be discovered.

An administrative inquiry is also known as a "local" or "public" inquiry, thus emphasising two of its characteristics. It is held in the vicinity of the matter in dispute and it is almost always open to the public, both to attend and, with reservations, to give evidence. As Parliament has come to find this procedure valuable, so it has increasingly made provision in Acts of Parliament for an inquiry to be held before the minister takes a particular policy decision. One has only to think of the minister's confirmation of compulsory purchase and clean air orders which are cases in point, since if there is an objection to the confirmation of the orders the minister must arrange for an inquiry to be held. Such inquiries are sometimes referred to as "statutory inquiries" since Parliament requires them to be held. Where on the other hand a minister has a choice under the statute whether or not to hold an inquiry, such an inquiry is called a "discretionary inquiry."

Administrative inquiries can be used in a vast number of situations, but the best known examples are those used in connection with the Town and Country Planning legislation, the making of compulsory purchase orders particularly in relation to new motorway or bypass routes and certain orders made under the Housing legislation.

The planning legislation originally allowed for an appeal from the refusal of permission by the local planning authority to the appropriate central government minister. Before giving his ruling the Minister would order an official, the inspector, to hold a local inquiry and report to him on the arguments presented. Problems and substantial delays arose because of the very large number of appeals which were made annually. In some cases the parties agreed, and may still do so, to an appeal by written representations but in the last ten years the system has been changed so that in the majority of appeals the decision will be given by the inspector himself following the inquiry. Only exceptionally, where the appeal is of considerable planning consequence, will the decision be reserved to the Minister, now the Secretary of State for the Environment. The interesting point is that where the inspector is deciding an appeal, he is acting as a tribunal acts, by resolving the matter.

Under the compulsory purchase and housing legislation there is a standard requirement that the minister, who has to confirm the orders, must arrange for an inspector to hold a local inquiry if there are objections. Following the inquiry and the submission of the inspector's report, the orders will be either confirmed or rejected or, which is frequently the case, confirmed subject to modifications.

Procedure

The person who holds the inquiry is known as the inspector, although the legislation always refers to him as "the person appointed." He is usually a professionally qualified civil servant on the staff of the ministry, but for some inquiries—for example those held by the Secretary of State for Education and Science into a proposal to acquire land for education purposes compulsorily—a professional lawyer, or surveyor, from private practice is appointed.

The procedure to be followed at the inquiry is laid down by statutory instrument for certain important inquiries; the most familiar being the Compulsory Purchase by Public Authorities (Inquiries Procedure) Rules 1976 (S.I. 1976 No. 746) and the Town and Country Planning (Inquiries Procedure) Rules 1974 (S.I. 1974 No. 419). Even where no procedural rules have been laid down the tendency is to copy the established practice, so that administrative inquiries follow a very similar pattern whatever may be the subject-matter of the inquiry. The rules ensure that the inquiry follows the methods of a court of law in that the inspector has the appearance of a judge, with parties or their legal representatives in turn presenting their view of the circumstances of the particular case. The persons who are called to give evidence are examined, cross-examined and re-examined; if appropriate, the site is visited, and the inspector then departs to write his report. In all inquiries, except that under the planning legislation where the inspector himself announces the result, the minister's decision is notified to the parties together with a copy or summary of the inspector's report and recommendation. The minister is not obliged to accept the recommendations of his inspector, although in the majority of cases he does do so. The minister must give reasons for his decision if requested (Tribunals and Inquiries Act 1971, s.12), and the reasons given must be adequate and reasonable.

There is no appeal from the minister's decision, but it may just be possible for a person not satisfied to obtain judicial review, by way of an order of prohibition or certiorari, from the Queen's Bench Divisional Court to quash the minister's decision, if it can be shown that the inquiry was not properly conducted or that there has been some other substantial flaw in the inquiry procedure. These orders are dealt with more fully at p. 104, below.

The term "inquiry"

As well as the administrative inquiry there are other kinds of inquiry occasionally used in the English legal system. One of these is the accident inquiry, held under statutory provisions, whenever a major accident involving public transport has occurred. The object is to make available an expert's report on the cause of the accident in an endeavour to prevent a recurrence. Another inquiry, less commonly called for, is that held under the Tribunals of Inquiry (Evidence) Act 1921, when Parliament agrees to institute an inquiry into a matter of urgent public importance. Finally there is nothing to prevent a minister from establishing an inquiry into any matter which he considers calls for investigation.

Development of the administrative inquiry system

The use of the administrative inquiry would seem to date from 1909, since when it has become a much-used method in the work of the government in this country. The commonsense basis on which it operates has made it acceptable both to politicians in office and to the public. This is because the minister is not bound by the findings of the inquiry, whilst the interested members of the public feel that the case has been properly considered by the person making the decision. As the years have passed, more and more statutes have either required, or permitted, that an inquiry shall take place before a particular decision is taken.

There has, of course, been criticism. Lord Hewart in *The New Des-*

potism (1929) found it "absurd" that one civil servant should hold an inquiry, and another should make the decision, disregarding the recommendations of the former. This criticism remains valid. Nonetheless the Donoughmore Committee on Ministers' Powers, which reported in 1932, and the Franks Committee on Administrative Tribunals and Enquiries, which reported in 1957 both found considerable merit in the system.

3. Arbitration

As an alternative to trial in the courts the commercial world has come to favour a process which is known as arbitration. This is the reference of a dispute for determination to a third party, who is usually not a judge or an officer of a court. The person appointed is known as an arbitrator, and the decision, which he comes to in the matter, is called an award. The arbitrator must conduct the hearing in a judicial manner and in the normal way his task will be governed by the provisions of the Arbitration Act 1950 as amended.

When an arbitration agreement is entered into it either specifies the arbitrator by name or, more commonly, it makes provision for the arbitrator to be appointed by the President for the time being of some appropriate professional body. This latter provision simply means that if an arbitration is found to be necessary, the parties then ask the office-holder named to exercise his power of appointment. It is possible for a judge to be appointed an arbitrator, and in the county court small claims are dealt with by the Registrar acting as an arbitrator (see p. 68).

The advantages, which are claimed for arbitration as a process compared with court proceedings are several in number. Generally arbitration is less expensive because, although the arbitrator has to be paid a fee, there is no court fee and no need to pay for the services of a solicitor and a counsel in the preparation of the pleadings and in the presentation of the case in court. Because the arbitration takes place in private and there is no formal court procedure, there is often no need for legal representation at all. The arbitration can be fixed at a time and place convenient for all the parties and there is no delay, no waiting for the case in the court list to be reached, with parties, witnesses and lawyers standing in the corridors of the court, and costs mounting hour by hour. Another important consideration is that the arbitrator chosen can be an expert in the particular field in which the dispute arises. The hearing can thus make rapid progress as compared with a similar hearing before a judge, where witnesses will have to be called to provide the judge with basic information before he can hope to get to the stage of understanding, let alone resolving, the dispute. The decision is immediate and, like the hearing, is private, and if necessary, as a last resort, the court can be called upon to enforce the arbitrator's award. With all these advantages it is not surprising that arbitration agreements are widely entered into and are generally found to be satisfactory.

There are, as might be expected, disadvantages which can be set up to temper the widespread enthusiasm for arbitration. It does not, for instance, follow that the process will necessarily be cheaper than litigation, because a professional man will charge a professional fee, and, furthermore, if the award should then be challenged in the courts, the costs of the arbitration will have been substantially wasted. To those who take the view that one gets what one pays for, the supposed advantages of quickness, cheapness, informality and lay representation are all in themselves likely to prove weaknesses. The arbitrator has long had a discretion to refer a legal problem arising in the course of the arbitration to a judge for determination, in the meantime adjourning the hearing. The arbitrator must conduct the arbitration in accordance with the rules of natural justice and in a judicial manner; he must give reasons for his award. Any misconduct on the part of the arbitrator can result in the Queen's Bench Divisional Court being asked to intervene to quash the award and require a rehearing.

Following a growing number of ill-founded applications for judicial review, leading to long delays in settling awards, Parliament passed the Arbitration Act 1979. This Act, which is comparatively complex, allows parties to exclude judicial review in certain defined instances and alternatively allows a right of appeal subject to stated conditions on any question of law arising out of an arbitrator's award. The court is given discretion in deciding whether to grant leave for an appeal on the point of law in question.

4. Judicial Supervision of Tribunals, Inquiries and Arbitrations

In addition to the appeal to the High Court on a point of law from the decisions of certain tribunals under section 13 of the Tribunals and Inquiries Act 1971 (see above, p. 98), all tribunals, inquiries and arbitrations are generally subject to the supervision of the High Court in certain matters. This supervision is exercised by means of the prerogative orders of certiorari, mandamus and prohibition, briefly mentioned in another chapter (at p. 43 above). Full discussion of these orders belongs properly to works on administrative law; here they are dealt with only in the broadest outline.

Certiorari

This order quashes unlawful decisions of a judicial nature by inferior courts and tribunals. It should be noted that "unlawful" does not mean "illegal" or even that the court or tribunal has made a mistake of law. "Unlawful" here relates to the manner in which the court or tribunal came to its decision: that is, either the court or tribunal had no jurisdiction, or it did not follow the rules of natural justice, or it made an error on the face of the record. The first of these may mean either that the court had no jurisdiction or that it had jurisdiction but acted in excess of it; the second may mean either that the court or tribunal was judge in its own cause (one most obvious instance of this, as well as being one of the earliest, is the case related by the eighteenth century writer Blackstone of the Chancellor of Oxford University in the time of Henry VI who was not allowed to try a case of trespass brought against himself), or that the court did not listen to both sides of the case (a leading case illustration of this is *Ridge* v. *Baldwin* (1964) in which a Chief Constable of Brighton was dismissed by a Watch Committee without any specific charge against him being formulated, and with virtually no chance of putting his case to the Watch Committee).

The third ground on which the order of certiorari may be granted, error on the face of the record, is of comparatively recent application and applies only to those tribunals which set out the reasons on which the decisions were based and in which there appears an error of law.

It should be noted that a person applying for this order must be in some way affected by the decision of which he is complaining, this is called having *locus standi*. Also the order does not lie against the decisions of domestic tribunals.

Mandamus

This order lies to compel any person, body or inferior court to carry out a statutory duty, such as set up a tribunal or grant a licence.

Prohibition

This order lies to prevent an inferior court or tribunal in a pending matter from exceeding its jurisdiction or from acting against the rules of natural justice. The law relating to this order is similar to that relating to certiorari except that the order cannot, for obvious reasons, be issued once the final decision of the court or tribunal has already been made.

Procedure

An application for judicial review is governed by the Rules of the Supreme Court Order 53 and section 31 of the Supreme Court Act 1981. The applicant needs the leave of a High Court Judge to apply for judicial review and the hearing is usually before a single judge. An indication of the growing importance of this procedure is that in 1981 100 applications were made, whereas in 1985 the corresponding figure was 1,230. Confirmation is also to be found in the recent creation of an Administrative Law Bar Association.

One important suggestion, contained in a 1986 lecture by Lord Justice Woolf, is that there should be created a new office of Director of Civil Proceedings to balance the role of the Director of Public Prosecutions. The Director of Civil Proceedings, it is proposed, would play an active part in bringing judicial review cases at public expense. This recognises that it is unrealistic for financial reasons to expect an individual, or even a small company, to take action against a public body in many instances where the outcome is uncertain.

10. Legal Aid And Advice

1. History

The legal aid and advice system is governed in detail by various Acts of Parliament supplemented by statutory instruments (see p. 120). The principal Act currently in force is the Legal Aid Act 1974 but this has been substantially amended and extended by later legislation.

The introduction of a state funded legal aid and advice scheme dates from 1949. The problems affecting society during and following upon the Second World War 1939–1945 made some such provision essential; not least because the previous position had been far from satisfactory relying substantially on voluntary assistance. The Legal Aid and Advice Act 1949 made provision for the gradual introduction and extension of a national legal aid and advice system. The administration of the system was placed in the hands of the Law Society where, despite criticism, it has remained. Consultation with the Lord Chancellor is fundamental since he is the Central Government Minister responsible and through his department he makes the statutory instruments which govern the operation of the scheme. The Law Society reports annually on its work in this sphere and there is also an independent Lord Chancellor's Advisory Committee on Legal Aid and Advice which publishes an annual report to the Lord Chancellor.

2. Legal Aid in Civil Cases

The Law Society has established 15 Area Committees, made up of solicitors and barristers, and a network of Local Committees, also made up of solicitors and barristers, which together with a number of salaried staff are the basis of the system. Every applicant for legal aid in a civil case must submit a detailed application to the Local Legal Aid Committee. The task of the Local Committee is to decide whether or not the applicant has reasonable grounds for taking, defending or being a party to the proceedings in question. The solicitors and barristers concerned determine this on the basis of their individual professional judgment, applying the standard of the reasonably prudent man of moderate means. If they decide in favour of granting legal aid, the committee issue a "legal aid certificate"; if they refuse a certificate an appeal generally lies to the Area Committee. If a legal aid applicant wishes in a case to appeal to the Court of Appeal or the House of Lords or the European Court of Justice, his application can only be dealt with by the Area Committee.

The legislation lays down that no legal aid is to be granted for cases involving defamation, whether libel or slander. Nor, until the Legal Aid Act 1979, did the scheme apply generally to tribunals and inquiries. Although the Lands Tribunal, the Commons Commissioners and the Employment Appeal Tribunal had already been brought within the main scheme, the 1979 Act allows "assistance by way of representation" before a tribunal or a statutory inquiry based on the legal advice and assistance provisions.

If a certificate is granted, the applicant must then be examined as to his financial means by an assessment officer of the Department of Health and Social Security. The object of this investigation is to discover the "disposable income" and the "disposable capital" of the applicant. In order to reach these figures the regulations allow subtractions to be made from the applicant's gross annual income and gross capital. These include from gross income such expenditure as maintenance of dependants, interest on loans, income tax, rates and rent; and in the case of capital, the value of the house in which the applicant resides and the value of his furniture. The full details are contained in the Legal Aid (Assessment of Resources) Regulations 1980.

In order to qualify for completely free legal aid the applicant must have a disposable income of less than £2,255 and a disposable capital of less than £3,000. At the other extreme if the applicant has a disposable income of more than £5,415 and a disposable capital of more than £4,710 legal aid is not normally available. In between these two extremes the applicant will be offered assistance on a sliding scale, but he will be required to make a contribution towards the cost of the action. There is a firm rule that the maximum that a legally-aided applicant can be called on to pay is all his disposable capital over £4,710 and one-quarter of the amount by which his disposable income exceeds £2,255 per annum.

Once the financial position has been ascertained the applicant receives an offer, setting out the contribution which he will have to make and the instalments by which he may pay it. He has 28 days in which to make up his mind whether or not to accept the offer. The practical advantage is that the applicant knows exactly what his commitment is.

If the applicant decides to accept the offer of legal aid he is invited to choose a solicitor from the panel of names kept by the Local Legal Aid Committee. If he is entitled to have counsel he will also have the right to select from the panel of names of barristers, who are willing to act in legal aid cases. Solicitors and barristers receive the taxed fees as allowed for their work in the county courts and in magistrates' courts. In the High Court and in the appeal courts they receive 90 per cent. of their normal profit costs, plus their disbursements. Originally the figure was 85 per cent. but it was increased to 90 per cent. in 1961. It is argued that the 10 per cent. which is not paid takes account of the fact that there are no bad debts, no delay in settlement and also that the legal aid scheme provides solicitors and barristers with a great deal more work than they would otherwise have; so that it deserves a discount!

All payments by the applicant are made to the legal aid fund and not to his solicitor. The fund receives these payments, together with the costs of successful cases and it also receives a substantial grant from the Exchequer to cover its deficit. The cost of the scheme in total is estimated to be £350 million in 1985/86.

One difficult problem is the position of the unassisted litigant who contests an action with an assisted litigant. If the assisted party wins then the unassisted party pays all the costs. If the unassisted party wins he may be unable to recover any costs from his opponent. Parliament recognised the injustice of this state of affairs in 1964 but the applicable statutory provisions are not generous—the Legal Aid Fund may be ordered to pay the whole or part of the costs if the proceedings at first instance are decided in favour of the unassisted party, the proceedings were instituted by the assisted party and the court is satisfied that the unassisted party will suffer "severe financial hardship" if the order is not made. In an appeal different statutory provisions allow an order for costs to be made against the Legal Aid Fund if the court considers it "just and equitable" that an order should be made.

3. Legal Advice and Assistance

The Legal Aid and Advice Act 1949 made provision for a legal advice service alongside the legal aid scheme. From a tentative beginning the scheme was substantially expanded in 1972 to provide qualified applicants with legal advice and assistance up to fixed financial limits. Known as the Green Form scheme, solicitors may give advice to, and do legal work for, a client up to a maximum currently of £50 (£90 in divorce matters) at the expense of the Legal Aid Fund subject to the finances of the client qualifying him for assistance. Provided the consent of the appropriate committee is first obtained the solicitor can proceed beyond the £50 limit and, if necessary, an application for a full legal aid certificate can be made later. The idea is to enable advice and assistance to be given straight-away without the delay involved in waiting for the grant of a certificate. Indeed in many cases the provision of legal advice may obviate any need for legal aid and dispose of the matter. The system has also been developed to provide "assistance by way of representation" at certain tribunals, so partly meeting criticism of the lack of legal aid provision in this area.

The financial qualifications under the scheme are to be found in the Legal Advice and Assistance (Financial Conditions) Regulations 1985. Eligibility depends upon having a disposable income, at present not exceeding £114 per week and disposable capital not exceeding £800. Free advice is available to those whose income is less than £54 per week; disposable incomes between £54 and £114 per week entail a contribution having to be made by the applicant.

4. Legal Aid in Criminal Cases

The critical difference between the civil and criminal statutory legal aid provisions is brought about by the much more pressing need for a speedy trial in criminal proceedings. In consequence, power is given to almost all criminal courts to grant a "legal aid order" to an applicant appearing before it, whenever it thinks it "desirable to do so in the interests of justice." In a House of Lords appeal in a criminal matter legal aid for the applicant is automatic and all the courts dealing with criminal cases have the power to grant legal aid. Where a charge of murder is involved a legal aid order must be made.

The order will usually permit the employment of a solicitor and a barrister, but it is possible for the order to be limited to a solicitor alone, as generally in cases in the magistrates' courts, or in rare instances to a barrister alone.

One problem which has attracted considerable attention is the inconsistency in the approach of magistrates to the exercise of the discretion to grant or refuse legal aid. Nationally there are very wide variations in the willingness of magistrates' courts to grant legal aid, but short of legislation to compel the making of the order there is no easy solution to the dilemma since all courts think they are right!

The financial arrangements inevitably have to follow trial rather than precede it. The court can require the assessment officer of the Department of Health and Social Security to examine the financial means of the person concerned, and as a result the court can order the assisted person to pay a reasonable contribution towards the cost of his legal aid, having regard to his commitments and his resources. Such an order is called a "contribution order." The financial obligation is regulated by the provisions of a statutory instrument but in general terms the amount of contribution payable lies in the discretion of the court.

The cost of criminal legal aid provision is approximately £150 million a year and rising rapidly.

The latest development in the field of criminal legal aid is the establishment of a nationwide duty solicitor scheme to operate in magistrates' courts. When fully operative defendants will have immediate access to legal advice at all times; the cost of the scheme will fall on the legal aid fund.

5. Praise and Criticism of the Legal Aid and Advice Scheme

Inevitably there have been conflicting voices raised in praise and criticism of the legal aid and advice system. To those who feel that there is a crying need for such a system the progress made has been all too slow. For reasons of national economy the provisions of the Legal Aid and Advice Act 1949 could only be introduced piecemeal over a number of years. Even now, although much talked of, only limited arrangements have been made for the extension of legal aid and advice to the tribunals and inquiries which are of great significance in the modern legal system.

Equally significant is the difficulty of governments in keeping the financial costs under control. The latest scrutiny of the administration of the scheme has fallen to a firm of private consultants, but previous examinations have not revealed much scope for savings. In 1986 the problem reached the courts with the Bar seeking judicial review of the Lord Chancellor's decision to impose an inflation linked fee rise. The Bar argued that payment for criminal legal aid work was indefensibly low.

An added problem is that the cost of litigation has increased so much that to be legally aided is of the first importance. A litigant with a legal aid certificate knows his or her maximum financial liability and is not, consequently, under any real pressure to bring the litigation to an end. Individuals who do not qualify for legal aid, unless they happen to be extremely wealthy, are at a marked disadvantage and will usually be ill-advised to tangle with an assisted opponent.

Another criticism is that the annual deficit of the Legal Aid Fund can cause the government to introduce changes intended to save money rather than to improve the legal system. The recent Efficiency Scrutiny by officials for the Lord Chancellor has emphasised this approach.

6. Local Law Centres

Research has shown that the crucial problem underlying the legal aid and advice system is that in certain highly populated urban areas there is a major unmet need for legal services, particularly among the poorer sections of the community. Not only is there a shortage of lawyers in these areas, there is also an unwillingness to consult such lawyers as are available.

Two contrary views are held as to a solution. One view is that incentives should be offered to practitioners to open offices in these localities. The thinking is that if profits are to be made then practitioners will appear. The radical view is that a drastic remedy is necessary. Salaried lawyers employed by the state are the only answer and these should operate nationally wherever circumstances so demand. Proponents of this view would argue that Local Law Centres are as necessary as Local Health Centres.

There were in 1985 some 60 Law Centres in being, funded by a variety of charitable and public bodies. The Centres have been able to show that they meet a considerable public need, with much work coming to them in areas such as social welfare law of little interest to the private practitioner. The Benson Report proposed the establishment of a national system of Citizens' Law Centres to be funded by central government. Actually, legal power for the Law Society to establish Law Centres with salaried staff has existed since 1972, but so far no attempt has been made to bring this power into operation.

Considerable anxiety is currently being expressed about the future existence of some Law Centres as a result of the abolition of the Greater London Council and the Metropolitan County Councils.

11. Sources of English Law

1. Origins

In every-day conversation it is quite common to hear someone say "You can't do that, it's against the law." One example is where a car driver slows down on entering a village because of the 30 miles per hour speed limit signs. If he were asked why he has slowed down he would doubtless point to the speed limit signs and explain that he does not want to be fined for breaking the law indicated by those signs. He is, of course, quite correct, but his approach is that of the layman; the lawyer pursues the matter a stage further by seeking to know the origin of the law. He would require to know the authority for the making of that law, and then he would go on to examine the conditions which have to be fulfilled before the law comes into force. For example, he would want to know exactly the form and colour which the signs must take, so as to be sure that the particular ones in question are effective, because unless they comply with the regulations, then it is not a breach of law not to comply with them. Similarly he would examine he procedure which had been followed involving the making of the order by the Highway Authority, and its submission to, and approval by, the Minister of Transport, to see that all the formalities had been complied with. This is because any failure in the procedural formalities would invalidate the order, and thus exceeding the limits specified would not be an offence. It can be seen that the lawyer's approach is a technical approach; in seeking to be satisfied of the authenticity of a law he is inevitably concerning himself with the sources, or origins of the law, which is the subject-matter of this chapter.

By the word "sources," in this context, is meant the various ways in which law in the English legal system can come into being, and will be recognised and given effect in the English courts. It is not always a simple matter to know whether some particular conduct is a breach of the law or not. The young girl who is coming home late from a dance and is afraid of the reception she will receive at home, suddenly decides, as an excuse, to tell a policeman that she has been accosted and possibly assaulted by a man. The police then waste time and money searching for a non-existent suspect. Has the girl committed a criminal offence? Only by a study of sources is it possible to decide.

At the present time the main sources of law reflect the complexity of modern society. Most new law is produced by Act of Parliament, but an equally important source of the law is the decisions of the judges in cases in the various courts, because the judge in each case is stating what the law is in the circumstances of the particular case and so in effect, making new law. Such a situation can only reach this degree of sophistication at a comparatively late stage in the development of a society; since for its effectiveness it presupposes that the legislation proposed by Parliament will be brought to the notice of the people it will affect, by means of the press, radio and television. It further assumes that this will be done in adequate time to enable Members of Parliament to be fully aware of the views of their constituents, and the interested pressure groups, before the legislation is passed and becomes law. Equally the importance of case decisions by judges can only be of practical value if there is a full system of law reporting, with the law reports being published immediately following the decision and being made easily accessible to lawyers and other interested parties.

Whilst no one would claim that the prevailing conditions are incapable of improvement, nonetheless new legislation and the more important case reports are accessible. The major problem with these two sources today is not accessibility so much as the tremendous bulk of law being produced in every branch of the law; more and more the maxim that "everyone is presumed to know the law"— "*ignorantia juris haud excusat*"—is demonstrably false. It is increasingly the case that the lawyer himself has to specialise in a particular branch or branches of the law in order to keep pace with developments. Outside his special field of knowledge he is likely to flounder nearly as badly as the layman. The only difference will be that the lawyer by his training will know where to look for the law, if he needs to pursue a legal point outside his field, whereas the layman will not.

The other accepted sources of law in the English legal system are custom and books of authority; neither of which is fractionally as important today as legislation and case law. In the building up of the system custom has however been, particularly during the earliest period, of first rate importance. This is because law, as it is first established, is derived from custom and therefore custom plays a major role in shaping the principles of the system. Books of authority fall into a different category mainly serving to elucidate legal points of difficulty in cases, either by reference to textbooks stating the law as it was, or from more recent academic treatises or articles.

Each of these sources of law will now be considered in detail.

2. Legislation

General

Most new law is made in documentary form by way of an Act of Parliament. In the British Constitution a vital doctrine is that of Parliamentary sovereignty which recognises that supreme power is vested in Parliament and that there is no limit in law to the law-making capacity of that institution. Consequently what Parliament passes in the form of an Act will be put into effect by the courts.

This acceptance by the courts of Parliament's supremacy is entirely a matter of history derived directly from the seventeenth century conflict between the Stuart Kings and Parliament. In that conflict the courts took the side of Parliament and one result of their joint success was that thereafter the courts have been prepared to acknowledge the supremacy of Parliament within its own sphere, whilst Parliament has readily allowed the independence of the judiciary to become an acknowledged factor in the Constitution. The contrast with the American system is however very marked in that in America the Supreme Court does have the power to overrule legislation as being "unconstitutional." No such power exists in the English legal system. So far as the English courts are concerned, an Act of Parliament, which has been passed by the accepted process, is the law and must be given effect. In *British Railways Board* v. *Pickin* (1974) an attempt was made to persuade the court to intervene, on the grounds that the Board had obtained powers in a private Act of Parliament by misleading Parliament. The Court of Appeal (Civil Division) was sympathetic to the complainant but on appeal the House of Lords refused to contemplate intervention holding that the complaint was entirely a matter for Parliament. The only role of the courts in relation to legislation is to "interpret" the statutory provisions to the circumstances of any given case. Just how this task of interpretation is approached is examined below.

The Queen in Parliament

First, however, it is essential that some brief explanation of the institution "Parliament" should be attempted; once this has been done, the documentary form of an Act of Parliament will be examined and thereafter the work of the judges in interpretation will be considered.

Parliament is made up of three constituent elements: the monarch, the House of Lords and the House of Commons. An Act of Parliament will thus in normal circumstances have the approval of all three elements, but it is possible, although it happens very rarely, that an Act of Parliament can be passed without the approval of the House of Lords. The monarch's place in Parliament has long become a formality. Despite the splendour of the throne in the House of Lords and the Queen's Robing Room and the Royal Gallery, the only occasion on which the monarch plays any part in the proceedings of Parliament is when she attends the opening of a new session of Parliament. At this ceremony the Queen, after making a formal entrance, reads the speech from the throne, which is the government's statement of its proposals for the coming session of Parliament. The speech is drawn up by the Prime Minister and his colleagues and does not in any way reflect the personal views of the monarch. The other activity of Parliament with which the Queen is concerned is the requirement that all legislation must receive the Royal Assent before it becomes law. At one time in English history the monarch had a discretion whether to say "Yes" or "No" to proposed legislation in the form "le roi/la reine le veult" or "le roi/la reine's s'avisera." The Royal Assent, to measures recommended to her by the House of Lords and the House of Commons, has not been refused since the reign of Queen Anne in 1707 and it is safe to say that it will never be refused. Under the provisions of the Royal Assent Act 1967 the monarch's approval is now notified to Parliament by the Speaker. It could however be given in person or by Lords Commissioners.

The House of Lords, which is now composed of hereditary peers of the realm together with life peers specially appointed to assist in the work of the House, has a very much more active part to play than has the monarch. Originally, the senior house, made up of persons who advised the monarch, it has in this century suffered a major diminution in its powers. By the Parliament Acts 1911 and 1949 the previous veto of the House of Lords over all legislation has been replaced by a one-year delaying power over public Bills, other than financial measures where there is no delaying power at all. Allowing for this lack of power the House of Lords continues to play a useful role in the consideration of Bills, by ensuring that the form of a Bill stands up to detailed scrutiny. It also serves as a debating chamber of national significance, and legislation of a technical and comparatively non-controversial kind can be introduced there.

From being in its origin the least important part of Parliament the

House of Commons, now made up of 650 democratically elected members, has become the most important element. The Prime Minister is always now drawn from the Commons, and the vast majority of government Ministers have seats there. Since the House of Lords has little more than a delaying power over legislation and in practice this is used very rarely, and as the monarch's role is a formal one, it can be seen that the majority party in the House of Commons can make law almost as it wishes. This power is of course controlled by the pressure of public opinion expressed through the press, radio and television and also by the views of members, both inside and outside Parliament, of the majority party itself.

Procedure

In order for a legislative measure to become an Act of Parliament and to be recognised as such by the judges, it has to undergo a traditional process. This process involves the measure being drafted in the appropriate legal terminology, usually by parliamentary counsel to the Treasury employed full-time as civil servants, and then presented in the House of Commons, or possibly the House of Lords, as a Bill. In the case of a Government Bill, the various clauses of the Bill will have been agreed by the department which has instructed the parliamentary counsel to draft the Bill.

Before the Bill becomes an Act of Parliament, and the clauses become sections, it must undergo five stages in each House. These are—First Reading; Second Reading; Committee Stage; Report Stage; Third Reading. The first reading is a formality: the second reading takes the form of a debate on the general principles of the measure; the committee stage sees the Bill examined in detail clause by clause; the report stage brings the House up to date with the changes which have taken place in the Bill at the committee stage; and the third reading allows for verbal changes only. These five stages can be taken very quickly, although in the normal way they will be spread over a period of weeks or even months. Much depends on the nature and length of the Bill, and how politically controversial it is.

Once the Bill with any amendments has been approved both by the House of Commons and the House of Lords it needs only the Royal Assent to become an Act of Parliament. Usually a number of Bills receive the Royal Assent individually through Lords Commissioners authorised expressly by the Queen. The result is that every Act of Parliament begins: "Be it enacted by the Queen's most Excellent Majesty, by and with the advice and consent of the Lords Spiritual and Temporal, and Commons, in this present Parliament assembled and by the authority of the same as follows. . . . " If, as rarely happens, an Act is passed without the consent of the Lords, the phrase referring to the consent of the Lords Spiritual and Temporal is omitted.

The Act of Parliament comes into effect when the Royal Assent is given, unless the Act contains its own starting date, or it has a provision which allows different parts of the Act to be brought into force at different times, by a Minister making a statutory instrument to that effect.

The form of an Act of Parliament
Language

Because an Act of Parliament creates new law, the language in which it is expressed must be precise in the extreme; in addition the provisions of every Act must be related to any existing legislation on the same subject. These factors combine to cause legislation to be most complicated and notoriously difficult for the layman to understand.

Although the earliest statutes were produced in Latin and French the change to English took place in the reign of Henry VII, and, whereas in earlier centuries statutes had long titles and often a lengthy preamble, since the Short Titles Act 1896 Acts of Parliament have been given a short title and preambles have become the exception.

Citation

The method of citing an Act of Parliament is now governed by the Acts of Parliament Numbering and Citation Act 1962. This Act stipulates that from 1963 every Act is to be given a chapter number for the year in which it receives the Royal Assent. This abolishes the centuries-old system by which Acts were given a chapter number for the session of the Parliament in question designated by the regnal year of the monarch. This system could produce difficulties as in 1937 which under the former system would be cited as "1 Edw. 8 and 1 Geo. 6." The present system is to refer to an Act by its short title and chapter number for the year in question: for example—The Prosecution of Offences Act 1985 (c. 23).

The method of citing private Bills involves local Bills having a chapter number in small Roman numerals, whilst personal Bills have the chapter number in small italicised Arabic figures. Church Assembly Measures are cited by their number.

The publication of an Act of Parliament is, under present circumstances, a matter for the Queen's Printer in the form of the Controller of Her Majesty's Stationery Office. When the Royal Assent has been given, the Queen's Printer has two vellum prints prepared and authenticated by the proper officers of each House, and one is deposited at the House of Lords and the other in the Public Records Office. In practice the Stationery Office makes new legislation available for sale to the public as soon as it has been given the Royal Assent. It also publishes annually a collection of the statutes for the year.

Public Bills and private Bills

A public Bill is legislation which affects the public at large, and applies throughout England and Wales.

A private Bill is legislation which affects a limited section of the population, either by reference to locality or by reference to a particular family or group of individuals. These are known respectively as local and personal Bills.

A private member's Bill is a public Bill introduced by a backbench Member of Parliament, as opposed to public Bills which are usually government legislation and introduced by the responsible minister.

Consolidation, Codification and Statute Law Revision

Consolidation is the process by which provisions in a number of Acts of Parliament are brought together and re-enacted in one Act. It is not a method for changing the law but it does make the law easier to find. In order to ease the passage of such measures Parliament passed the Consolidation of Enactments (Procedure) Act 1949 and this enables the Lord Chancellor to submit to a joint committee of Parliament a memorandum showing how the new Act proposes to incorporate the existing statutory provisions. If the joint committee is satisfied and recommends acceptance the new Act should pass the necessary stages in both Houses without undue delay and without a long debate. The procedure is now much used and every year several such Acts find their way on to the Statute Book. In 1985, for example, the legislation concerning companies was consolidated in the Companies Act 1985 (c. 6). This Act contains 747 sections and 25 Schedules.

Codification is the term used for an Act of Parliament which brings together all the existing legislation and case law and forms a complete restatement of the law. It can involve changes in the law and is thus one method of law reform. For this reason there is no simplified Parliamentary procedure.

The Law Commission, which was set up under the Law Commissions Act 1965, has, as one of its responsibilities, to keep under review all the law with a view to its systematic development and reform including, in particular, the codification of the law. It is consequently working at the present time on possible legislation which will, at some future time, codify particular branches of the law. (See p. 185).

Statute Law Revision is the procedure under which obsolete provisions in statutes are repealed and legislation is kept up to date. This is now a matter for the Law Commission which has overall responsibility for advising the repeal of obsolete and unnecessary enactments. The latest legislation is the Statute Law (Repeals) Act 1986.

Delegated legislation

This is the name given to law made in documentary form by subordinate authorities acting under the authority of Parliament. Such legislation can take the following forms:

Orders in Council

Parliament sometimes permits the government through Her Majesty in Council to make law by way of an Order in Council. This is particularly true where an emergency is imminent; for example, under the Emergency Powers Act 1920 the Crown can, in the stated circumstances, by Proclamation declare a state of emergency. The Crown can then by Order in Council issue regulations for securing the essentials of life to the community. An Order in Council requires the formality of a meeting of the Privy Council in the presence of the Queen. The quorum is three members and the signature of the Queen must be countersigned by the Clerk of the Privy Council.

Statutory instruments

A more common form of delegated legislation is the power frequently given to Ministers of the Crown to make law for specified purpose. The document containing this law is called a statutory instrument and some 2,000 are issued every year. As each one is published it is given a number for the year, for example the Value Added Tax Tribunal Rules is S.I. 1986 No. 590. Statutory instruments have become of major importance as a source of law. Some central government departments are responsible for large numbers of statutory instruments. For example those relating to Transport fill more than 250 pages of one of the 24 volumes of the collected statutory instruments.

By-laws

Parliament has long been willing to delegate to local authorities and certain other public bodies the power to make local laws limited to their particular functions. Thus the district local authorities and the London boroughs can make town laws, or by-laws, for "the good rule and government" of their areas. Even so the authority has to obtain confirmation of the by-laws from the named central government minister before the by-laws take effect. The power to make by-laws also belongs to British Rail and the British Airports Authority.

Statutory interpretation
Rules for statutory interpretation

Inevitably disputes arise as to the meaning or application of legislation, and the task of the judges in this context is, therefore, described as that of statutory interpretation. To guide the judges, Parliament has provided them with the general assistance of the Interpretation Act 1978, and often the additional assistance of an interpretation section in the statute itself. The Interpretation Act 1978 in one of its better-known sections provides that "unless the contrary intention appears (a) words importing the masculine gender include the feminine (and vice-versa) (b) words in the singular include the plural, and words in the plural include the singular." Even with the help of the Interpretation Act and such definitions as are offered by the particular statute which is being considered by the court, the judges are constantly faced with cases which turn on the interpretation of a word or phrase in a statute for which no adequate definition is provided by the legislature. The vast majority of Court of Appeal and House of Lords cases concern statutory interpretation. As a result of the many decisions of the courts in such cases there are a number of rules, known as the rules of statutory interpretation, which appear to be the guidelines used by the judges.

The first principle is that the judge should apply the words according to their "ordinary, plain and natural meaning." This is known as the literal rule, the application of "*litera legis.*"

In *Cresswell* v. *B.O.C. Ltd.* (1980) the applicant sought rating exemption on the grounds that his fish farm fell within the statutory provisions governing agricultural buildings and land. The linguistic consideration in the last resort was whether "fish" were "livestock." Applying the literal rule the Court of Appeal was unanimous in saying No. As a direct consequence of this decision fish farms were expressly given rating exemption in the Local Government, Planning and Land Act 1980.

A second principle which is derived from the literal rule, and which has become known as the golden rule, is that the literal application need not be applied, if to do so would lead to absurdity or to inconsistency within the statute itself. An outstanding example of the golden rule occurred in *Re Sigsworth* (1935), where a man was found to have murdered his mother. In the statute dealing with the distribution of the mother's estate it was laid down that the estate was to be distributed amongst "the issue." The son was her only child. The judge held that the common law rule that a murderer cannot take any benefit from the estate of a person he has murdered prevailed over the apparently clear words of the statute. The same principle seems to have been applied in the death of the playwright Joe Orton where a substantial legacy had been left to the person responsible for his death and Orton was treated as intestate so far as the legacy was concerned.

A third principle is that if the literal or golden rules fail to assist the judge, he is entitled to consider the "mischief" rule. This rule, which was first settled in *Heydon's Case* in 1584, allows the judge to consider (1) what was the common law, (2) what was the defect or mischief in the common law, (3) what remedy Parliament in the legislation has provided for the defect. Here a judge is entitled to examine existing legislation and case law before coming to his decision, with the intention that his ruling will "suppress the mischief and advance the remedy." In *Kruhlak* v. *Kruhlak* (1958) the court held, in connection with affiliation proceedings, that a married woman with no husband to support her is "a single woman" for the purposes of that legislation. The mischief at which the statute in that case was aimed was the situation of an illegitimate child with no means of support. This rule is sometimes referred to as interpretation *"ratio legis"* as distinct from interpretation *"litera legis."*

The court is not easily persuaded to reject the plain words of the statute. Lord Scarman in *Stock* v. *Frank Jones (Tipton) Ltd.* (1978) explained that "if the words used by Parliament are plain there is no room for the anomalies test, unless the consequences are so absurd that without going outside the statute, one can see that Parliament must have made a drafting mistake . . . but mere manifest absurdity is not enough; it must be an error (of commission or omission) which in its context defeats the intention of the Act."

Other rules and presumptions

As well as these major rules associated with statutory interpretation there are a number of other rules and presumptions, which the judges have introduced to help them in their task of interpretation.

One such minor rule is that where, in a statute, specific words are followed by general words, the general words must be given effect in the light of the foregoing specific words. This is called the *"eiusdem generis"* rule. An example is *Hobbs* v. *C. G. Robertson Ltd.* (1970)

where the Court of Appeal had to construe the following phrase concerning the provision of goggles in the Construction (General Provision) Regulations 1961:—"breaking, cutting, dressing or carving of stone, concrete, slag or similar materials"—to circumstances where a workman injured an eye, through the splintering of brickwork from a chimney breast which he was required to move. The court applied the *eiusdem generis* rule in holding that brick was not "a similar material" to stone, concrete or slag; the provision of goggles was therefore not compulsory and the workman's claim failed. A connected rule is that where in a statute there is a list of specified matters, which is not followed by general words, then only the matters actually mentioned are caught by this provision of the Act. The Latin phrase for this is *"expressio unius exclusio alterius."* In *R*. v. *Inhabitants of Sedgley* (1831) a statutory provision for rating occupiers of "lands, houses, tithes and coal mines" was held not to apply to any other kind of mine. The rule *"noscitur a sociis"* means that where two or more words follow each other in a statute, they must be taken as related for the purpose of interpretation. For example, in *Inland Revenue Commissioners* v. *Frere* (1965) the House of Lords held that in the relevant statute the phrase "interest, annuities or other annual payments" the word interest meant annual interest.

It is accepted practice that a statute must be taken as a whole. Consequently it follows that a judge must relate a word or phrase in a statute to its place in the context of the whole measure.

Other presumptions are that:

   (i) no change in the existing law is presumed beyond that expressly stated in the legislation;

   (ii) the Crown is not bound unless the Act specifically makes it so;

   (iii) legislation is not intended to apply retrospectively unless this is expressly stated to be the case;

   (iv) any change in the law affecting the liberties of the subject must be expressly and specifically stated;

   (v) any liability for a criminal offence must be on the basis of fault, unless the words of the statute clearly intend otherwise;

   (vi) the legislation applies throughout the United Kingdom unless an exemption for Scotland or Northern Ireland is stated. Because Scotland, in particular, has its own legal and local government system, it is common for Parliament to legislate for Scotland separately;

   (vii) if the provisions of two Acts appear to be in conflict the court will endeavour to reconcile them, since there is no presumption of implied repeal. if reconciliation is not possible, logic demands that the later provision be given effect.

Extrinsic and intrinsic aids

It has become a firm rule that a judge must limit himself to the Act of Parliament in question. He must not, in his task of interpretation, seek assistance from other sources, known as extrinsic aids, such as the *Hansard* reports of what took place in Parliament in the course of the enactment of the legislation in question. The reason for this rule is that the judge is not concerned with the intentions of Parliament, he is only required to have regard to the law which Parliament has actually passed. Because of this rule the judge is unable, theoretically, to make use of parliamentary debates, reports of committees or commissions or what the government Ministers involved have said about the measure. This rule, that no extrinsic aids will be used, ensures that Parliament has a complete obligation to express itself precisely when making new law.

The judge is, however, entitled to find assistance from the intrinsic aids contained in the statute itself; these include the long title, the preamble, headings, which may be prefixed to a part of the Act, and Schedules, which are part of the Act although they do not affect words used in the body of the Act unless these are ambiguous. Punctuation and marginal notes are not generally treated an an effective part of the Act.

Different considerations apply in the case of a statute which incorporates an international convention. Here exceptionally the court must have regard to the full background and reference may be made to relevant material which explains the provisions in the convention. For a recent discussion by the House of Lords of this matter, see *Fothergill* v. *Monarch Airlines Ltd.* (1980) where the amount involved was £16.50 and the linguistic problem was whether "damage" included "loss."

It can be gathered from the strictness of the judicial approach that if the words of a statute fail to deal with a particular situation, there is no power in a court to fill the gap. This absence of provision is known as "*casus omissus,*" and in general the principle requires Parliament to pass a new statute to make good the deficiency. Lord Simonds in *Magor and St Mellors R.D.C.* v. *Newport Corporation* (1952) said on this point "the power and duty of the court to travel outside them (the words of a statute) on a voyage of discovery are strictly limited. . . . If a gap is disclosed, the remedy lies in an amending Act."

This view is unrealistic. Generally Parliament, save in taxation cases, is very slow to amend faulty legislation; an example is the breathalyser law where judges have been pointing out weaknesses in the legislation for years. However in recent years the House of Lords seems to have grasped the nettle and become much more willing to give a purposive construction to legislation. In the *Fothergill Case* (above) Lord Diplock is explicitly critical of Lord Simonds approach and lays the blame for unsatisfactory rules of statutory interpretation on the judges' "narrowly semantic approach to statutory construction, until the last decade or so."

Criticism

Not unnaturally, considerable criticism has been expressed from time to time at the inflexible attitude of some judges in the task of statutory interpretation. In view of the difficulty of using language with an exactness which covers every conceivable situation, including the future, critics claim that the task of construction would be better done if judges took off their blinkers and considered all the circumstances which are relevant to the interpretation of the legislation in the particular case.

Another, in some ways more serious, criticism is that there is a lack of consistency in the application of the rules. It is suggested that a judge may use whichever rule leads to the result which he wishes to achieve; on one occasion he will rely on the literal rule, whereas on another he will reject the literal rule and apply the mischief rule.

The Law Commission in a report in 1969 called "The Interpretation of Statutes" criticised the narrow approach of the judges and recommended (i) that when Parliament produces an Act it should also provide what the Commission calls Explanatory Material; and (ii) that Parliament should enact a statute to specify what aids of interpretation the court might look at. It suggests the inclusion of reports and command papers on which the legislation is based, punctuation and marginal notes within the Act and relevant treaties and documents; it does not, however, propose that reports of proceedings in Parliament should be included. No action has been taken on this report.

Another consideration is that the judicial approach to statutory interpretation in the English legal system is completely at odds with the methods used in the European Court of Justice where the approach to construction is very flexible.

3. Case Law

General

Legislation as a source of law has been given pride of place because, at the present time, most new law is the work of Parliament, either directly by Act of Parliament or indirectly through delegated legislation. On the other hand, case law, the source of law now to be considered, is historically older than legislation and it continues, as it has done through the centuries, to make an important contribution to the English legal system.

By case law is meant the decisions of judges laying down legal principles derived from the circumstances of the particular disputes coming before them. From earliest times in the history of the legal system continuing attention has been paid to the reasoned judgments expounded by judges to justify their case decisions. When Chaucer in the Prologue to the *Canterbury Tales*, written about 1380, was describing the Serjeant-at-Law, he expressly states that this barrister was an exceptional lawyer, because he knew all the important case law decisions since the Norman Conquest. From this description it can be seen that even in medieval England the decisions of the judges were of great importance.

The doctrine of judicial precedent—meaning

The reason why such importance is attached to case decisions is explained by this doctrine of judicial precedent, which is also known as "*stare decisis*" (to stand upon decisions). This doctrine, in its simplest form, means that when a judge comes to try a case, he must always look back to see how previous judges have dealt with previous cases (precedents) which have involved similar facts in that branch of the law. In looking back in this way the judge will expect to discover those principles of law which are relevant to the case which he has to decide. The decision which he makes will thus seek to be consistent with the existing principles in that branch of the law, and may, in its turn, develop those principles a stage further.

Because the branches of English law have been gradually built up over the centuries, there are now some 300,000 reported case decisions available, so that the task of discovering relevant precedents and achieving consistency is by no means simple. An added factor, and one of the greatest importance, is that the standing of a precedent is governed by the status of the court which decided the case. Decisions of the House of Lords are obviously to be treated with the greatest respect, whereas a decision of a county court judge has normally limited effect. This quite common sense approach has developed into a rigid system under which precedents of the senior courts, if found to be relevant to the facts of a particular case, are treated as "binding" on the lower courts, so that the judge in the lower court must follow the reasoning and apply it to the case before him. He is thus obliged to decide the case in accordance with binding judicial precedent.

The doctrine of judicial precedent—operation

In order to understand the way in which this doctrine works in practice, it is necessary to consider the application of it through the hierarchy of the courts.

The House of Lords

As the supreme appeal court in matters civil and criminal, decisions of the House of Lords are binding on all the courts lower in the hierarchy. This is so not only where the facts of the later case are identical, which will be very rare, but also where the facts of the case call for the application of the same legal principle as in the House of Lords case. Until 1966, by reason of the binding nature of judicial precedent, a decision of the House of Lords, once made, remained binding on itself, as well as on all the courts lower in the structure. In 1966, by a formal Practice Statement, the House of Lords judges announced that in future they would not regard themselves as necessarily bound by their own previous decisions. The Practice Statement said: "Their Lordships regard the use of precedent as an indispensable foundation upon which to decide what is the law and its application to individual cases. It provides at least some degree of certainty upon which individuals can rely in the conduct of their affairs, as well as a basis for orderly development of legal rules. Their Lordships nevertheless recognise that too rigid adherence to precedent may lead to injustice in a particular case and also unduly restrict the proper development of the law. They propose, therefore, to modify their present practice and, while treating former decisions of this House as normally binding, to depart from a previous decision when it appears right to do so. In this connection they will bear in mind the danger of disturbing retrospectively the basis on which contracts, settlements of property and fiscal arrangements have been entered into and also the especial need for certainty as to the criminal law. This announcement is not intended to affect the use of precedent elsewhere than in this House."

There have not been many instances since the 1966 Practice Statement of the House of Lords departing from a previous decision. In *Herrington* v. *British Railways Board* (1972) the court revised a long-standing legal principle concerned with the duty of care owed to a child trespasser; and in *Miliangos* v. *George Frank (Textiles) Ltd.* (1976) it reversed a rule that a judgment could only be given in sterling. In *R.* v. *Shivpuri* (1986) the House of Lords departed from a decision given only one year earlier when reconsidering the law relating to criminal attempts.

The Court of Appeal

The Civil Division of the Court of Appeal by its decisions binds all the courts in the structure except the House of Lords. Its decisions in civil cases are of very great importance in the system. The Court of Appeal does bind itself for the future, according to the decision in *Young* v. *Bristol Aeroplane Co.* (1944); although it may escape if (i) a later decision of the House of Lords applies; (ii) there are previous conflicting decisions of the Court of Appeal; or (iii) where the previous decision was made *"per incuriam,"* *i.e.* in error, because some relevant precedent or statutory provision was not considered by the court.

This statement of theory has produced considerable conflict in its application on a number of occasions in recent years. This is not surprising in that Lord Denning M.R., when the senior judge of the court, was not convinced of the wisdom of so rigid a system and his colleagues tended to put differing emphasis on the application of the rules depending on the circumstances of the case. An interesting example of an expedient approach to the problem is *Tiverton Estates Ltd.* v. *Wearwell* (1975) where one division of the Court of Appeal (Civil Division) was able to convince itself that it need not follow *Law* v. *Jones* (1974) which had been decided by another division of the court only six months earlier. The case dealt with a property law point of great practical importance.

The Criminal Division of the Court of Appeal does not consider itself always bound by its own decisions. Where the liberty of the subject is concerned the court feels itself free to overrule a previous decision if it appears that in that decision the law was misunderstood or misapplied.

The High Court

Decisions of a single judge in the three divisions of the High Court are binding on the circuit judge but not on other High Court judges. If a High Court judge is presented with a precedent from a previous High Court case he will treat the precedent as "persuasive," and not as "binding." This means that he will consider the reasoning of his brother judge and will probably follow it; but he does not have to do so. Decisions by a Divisional Court are binding on judges of the same Division sitting alone.

The county court

The decisions of circuit judges have no binding effect. In practice very few of them are even reported. This is because they are generally concerned with fact and only a limited number of cases involve a point of law of general interest.

Terminology
Binding and persuasive
It has already been explained that depending on the status of the court a precedent may be binding or it may be persuasive. The latter term applies to precedents which derive from a court at the same level, as, for example, when one High Court judge considers an earlier case decision by another High Court judge. On the other hand precedents which come from the Judicial Committee of the Privy Council (see p. 51) or from countries within the common law jurisdiction, like Canada and Australia, are also said to be persuasive.

Other terms
Where a judge finds that a precedent to which he is referred is not strictly relevant to the facts of the case with which he is concerned, he is said to "distinguish" that case. As such the case is not binding upon him.

If, on the other hand, the judge holds that a precedent is relevant, and applies it, he is said to "follow" the reasoning of the judge in the earlier case.

When an appeal court is considering a precedent, it may "approve" the principle of law established in the case, or it may "disapprove" the precedent. It can "overrule" the principle of law established in a precedent if the case was decided by a court junior in status to it.

A decision is said to be "reversed" when a higher court, on an appeal, comes to the opposite conclusion to the court whose order is the subject of the appeal.

Ratio decidendi and obiter dicta
The system of judicial precedent causes judgments to be carefully scrutinised, and one result of this is that it has been discovered long since that every judgment falls into two parts. There is first the vital reasoning which leads the judge to decide the particular issue in favour of the plaintiff or the defendant, the reason for the decision or "*ratio decidendi*" as it is known; and then the remainder of the judgment, which deals by way of explanation with cases cited and legal principles argued before the court, is called "*obiter dicta*" or things said by the way. The whole of a dissenting judgment is "*obiter dicta*."

It is the "*ratio*" of a decision, which constitutes the binding precedent; or "*rationes*" if there is more than one reason. So that when in a case a judge is referred to a precedent, the first task of the court is to decide what was the *"ratio"* of that case, and to what extent it is relevant to the principle to be applied in the present case. Whilst an *"obiter dictum"* is not binding, it can, if it comes from a highly respected judge, be very helpful in establishing the legal principles in the case under consideration.

So important is it that a judgment should be accurately recorded that, before publication in the "official" law reports, judges are asked to check for accuracy the court reporter's version of the judgment.

Advantages and disadvantages of the doctrine of judicial precedent

The main advantages of the doctrine are that it leads to consistency in the application and development of the principles in each branch of the law, and by virtue of this characteristic it enables lawyers to forecast with reasonable certainty what the attitude of the courts is likely to be to a given set of facts. The system is flexible in that it can find an answer to any legal problem, and it is essentially practical in that the courts are perpetually dealing with actual circumstances. It must also be said that one result of the recording of cases over the centuries is that the tremendous wealth of detail leads to considerable precision in the principles established in each field of law.

To balance these advantages, critics of judicial precedent will argue that the way in which the discretion of the judge is restricted is undesirable, and can lead to a judge, who wishes to escape from a precedent, drawing illogical distinctions. Added to this is the difficulty, which can occur in some appeal court decisions, of discovering exactly what principle led to the particular decision. This has been known to be the case when the House of Lords decides an appeal by a majority vote of 3 to 2, and the three judges in the majority appear to arrive at their decision for different reasons! An example of this difficulty is *Harper* v. *National Coal Board* (1974) where the Court of Appeal was for this reason, unable to discover the *ratio decidendi* of the House of Lords' decision in *Dodd's Case* (1973).

A final factor, which is a practical problem, is that there are so many cases being dealt with each year—the total number of civil proceedings begun in 1985 was over two and a half million—that inevitably there is increasing complexity in each branch of the law. The sheer bulk of cases on commercial or criminal law is almost overwhelming and causes textbooks to become increasingly specialised and substantial. Even so it can well happen that a case of importance is not reported and so may go unnoticed for some considerable time. Such a case remains a precedent.

Law reports

A direct result of the application of the doctrine of judicial precedent is that cases must be properly reported and that the published reports must be readily accessible. One consequence is that in the English legal system there is a vast collection of law reports, of varying degrees of accuracy, stretching back over the centuries.

The earliest case summaries were collected in manuscript form in what became known as the *Year Books*. These seem to have been privately prepared and circulated among the judges and leading barristers. It is impossible now to know exactly how the system then operated, but it is obvious from Chaucer's Serjeant-at-Law that considerable attention was paid to previous case decisions.

With the invention of printing the production of law reports for sale to the legal profession, between the sixteenth and nineteenth centuries, became common practice. These reporters varied widely in their accuracy and reliability, but their law reports remain available, and have now been republished in a series of 176 volumes.

Since 1865 law reporting has been placed on a different basis although it remains a matter for private enterprise. A Council was set up in that year and in 1870 was incorporated as the Incorporated Council of Law Reporting. It consists of representatives of the Law Society and the Inns of Court and publishes what have come to be treated as the official *Law Reports*. These are in four series: Appeal cases (A.C.), Queen's Bench (Q.B.), Chancery (Ch.) and Family (Fam.). The reports are published some considerable time after the judgment has been given, but are regarded as authentic. The Council also publishes the *Weekly Law Reports* (W.L.R.), which are available sooner, approximately six months after the decision, and there is another series called the *All England Law Reports* (All E.R.), which is also published weekly by a firm of law publishers. As well as these full reports a number of law magazines carry summaries of recent case decisions, whilst *The Times* newspaper carries full reports of the most important cases actually in progress. Certain professional publications, like the *Estates Gazette*; the *Justice of the Peace*; and *Knight's Local Government Reports*, publish case reports of interest to their particular readers. So that all in all law reporting has become a vital characteristic of the system.

It has long been the practice for the work of law reporting to be done by barristers who attend the court throughout the hearing of the case. The preparation of a law report, and in particular the head-note summarising the relevant facts and the legal principles arising, is a specialised task.

Conclusion

It will now be apparent that case law is, and has always been, a major source of English law. Some branches of the law, as will be seen in Chapter 12, have been painstakingly built up over the years by the gradual application of case decisions; contract and tort in particular are substantially derived from the principles established by hundreds of judgments in actual cases. Even those branches of the law which are based on statute are nonetheless vitally affected by case decisions, since these decisions construe the statutory provisions in question.

4. Custom

History

In the development of the English legal system the common law was derived from the different laws of the existing Anglo-Saxon tribal groups in, for example, Kent and Wessex. The term "common law" emphasises the point. As England became one nation, with one king and one government, so the laws of the Anglo-Saxon regions had to be adapted into a national law common to the whole country. Since the difference between the regions stemmed from their different customary laws it is no exaggeration to say that custom was the principal original source of the common law.

In this historical sense custom, as the basis of common law, continues to play a part over the medieval period. In such a branch of the law as the criminal law it is necessary for a national system to be introduced at once; but in property law there is not the same apparent need for consistency, and so regional differences in, for example, succession to property, continue for centuries. Eventually, in the cause of uniformity, Parliament intervenes and legislation imposes a national system.

Customs thus are absorbed into the legal system, sometimes in the form of legislation and sometimes, particularly in the earliest period, by the judges giving decisions in cases which are based on custom. The gradual result is that custom virtually disappears as a creative source of law. An exception exists at the present day on a limited scale for cases where the courts can be convinced that a particular local custom applies. Usually in such cases custom is pleaded as a defence as permitting the conduct in question. The courts will only accept such a plea, under the stringent conditions set out below.

The term "custom"

There are three generally accepted meanings of the term "custom."

"General custom"

This is the common law built up on the basis of the previously existing customs of the various regions of Anglo-Saxon England. The most famous expression of this view is that contained in Blackstone's *Commentaries* (1765) where he writes of "the first ground and chief corner-stone of the laws of England, which is general immemorial custom, or common law, from time to time declared in the decisions of the courts of justice." It seems to be accepted now that general custom is no longer a creative source of law, because it has long since been absorbed into legislation or into case law.

"Mercantile custom"

By the very nature of overseas trade, the persons who engage in it gradually build up their own business principles in such matters as, for example, methods of payment. These practices, becoming internationally accepted, are known as mercantile customs and eventually are accepted into every national system as part of that country's commercial law. As these customs develop so the law will take notice of the changes and will formalise them as laws.

"Local custom"

This is the term used where a person claims that by virtue of a local custom he is entitled to a right of way, a right of common or a right to use land for a particular purpose, and can have his claim adjudicated upon judicially. If the claim is accepted by the court the local custom is treated as being local law.

Conditions for legal recognition of a local custom

From what Blackstone's *Commentaries* state, and from later decided cases, it would seem that the following conditions must all be complied with before a local custom will be recognised as law.

1. The customs must have existed from "time immemorial." By the Statute of Westminster 1275 the law has fixed the first year of the reign of Richard 1, 1189, as the date of "time immemorial." It would obviously be impossible for the person claiming the custom to show conclusively that it existed in 1189. Consequently the courts will accept a presumption that, if it can be shown that the custom has existed throughout the life-time of the oldest inhabitant in the locality, then it will be presumed that it has been in existence since 1189. The onus of rebutting the presumption falls on the party who denies the custom. Sometimes he can do this by showing, for example, that the custom has come into existence under Parliamentary legislation

at some time since 1189. In *Simpson* v. *Wells* (1872) the claimant was defeated because the "custom" in question came into existence under a fourteenth-century statute.

2. The custom must be limited to a particular locality and it must be certain as to exactly what the limits of its subject-matter are, and certain too as to the persons to whom it applies. The custom must be obligatory in the sense that the parties have no choice in its exercise.

3. The claim to the custom must have existed continuously and the custom must be a reasonable one judged from the standpoint of the law. In *Wyld* v. *Silver* (1963) the court held that a customary right could not be lost by disuse or waiver, but only by an Act of Parliament. On the question of reasonableness a claim by a clergyman to a customary fee of 13s. 0d. on performing the marriage ceremony failed because in 1189 13s 0d. would have been a very large amount quite beyond the ability to pay of the majority of the community (*Bryant* v. *Foot* (1868)).

4. The custom must have been exercised openly; "*nec per vim, nec clam, nec precario*," *i.e.* not by force, not secretly, not with special permission. A claim to a custom entitling a fisherman to the annual grant of a licence to fish in an oyster fishery failed, because the fact of the issue of a licence meant with a special permission (*Mills* v. *Colchester Corporation* (1867)).

5. A custom must be consistent with the existing law and must not be in conflict with statute or common law. This is well illustrated by the eighteenth century case of *Noble* v. *Durell* (1789) where a claim to a local custom that a pound of butter sold at a certain market should weigh 18 ounces failed, because a seventeenth century statute had enacted that a pound was to be taken as 16 ounces.

A case which saw the fulfilment of all these conditions, and the court therefore accepted the local custom as law, was *Mercer* v. *Denne* (1904). Local fishermen at Walmer in Kent had, for generations, dried their fishing nets upon a particular piece of ground. As a result of a change in ownership of the land a dispute over this practice arose which was decided by the court in favour of the fishermen.

Then in 1967 in *Beckett* (*A.F.*) *Ltd.* v. *Lyons* a claim of custom was advanced by certain residents of Hartlepool, County Durham, in claiming the right to collect sea-coal from the sea shore there. The Court of Appeal rejected the claim but it had succeeded before the judge at first instance. Other more recent instances in which custom was argued include *Egerton* v. *Harding* (1975) where the case concerned an alleged custom for an owner to fence against animals on common land; and *New Windsor Corporation* v. *Mellor* (1975) where the local authority were restrained from utilising land called "Bachelor's Acre," which customarily had been used for centuries for recreation by the local inhabitants.

5. Books of Authority

General

The fundamental division, which is drawn in connection with legal books as a source of law, is into those of considerable antiquity and those of recent origin. Both categories are of importance and have a part to play in the system, but only the books of antiquity can strictly be regarded as a source of law.

Books of authority

In this category fall certain ancient textbooks, any one of which by long standing judicial tradition, can be accepted as an original source of law. Not all old textbooks are so treated, only a limited number in each major branch of the law being universally accepted by the judges and the legal profession as having achieved the necessary standing. These books are then accepted by the courts as authoritative statements of the law at the time when they were written. Whether a particular book is accepted as authoritative, depends on its professional reputation; there is no way of knowing other than by a study of professional practice.

The following works, most of which were written by judges, are accepted as books of authority—

Glanvill: *De Legibus et Consuetudinibus Angliae,* c. 1189: authoritative on the land law and the criminal law of the twelfth century.

Bracton: *De Legibus et Consuetudinibus Angliae,* c. 1250: mainly commentaries on the forms of action with case illustrations. A major study of the common law.

Littleton: of *Tenures,* c. 1480: a comprehensive study of land law.

Fitzherbert: *Natura Brevium,* c. 1534; a commentary on the register of writs.

Coke: *Institutes of the Laws of England,* 1628: an attempted exposition in four parts of the whole of English law.

Hale: *History of the Pleas of the Crown,* 1736 (60 years after Hale's death): the first history of the criminal law.

Hawkins: *Pleas of the Crown,* 1716: a survey of the criminal law and criminal procedure.

Foster: *Crown Cases,* 1762; authoritative within its scope, which is concerned with the criminal law.

Blackstone: *Commentaries on the Laws of England,* 1765: a survey of the principles of English law in the mid-eighteenth century intended for students.

From the time of Blackstone on, writers of legal textbooks have fallen into the second category, that is those of recent origin.

Two examples of modern cases where reference has had to be made to these books of authority are: (i) *R.* v. *Button* (1966) where the House of Lords had to decide whether or not the crime of causing an affray could be charged where the disturbance took place on private premises instead of in a public place. Lord Gardiner, the then Lord Chancellor, giving the judgment of the House of Lords that it did constitute the crime, recorded the views on the point at issue of a long list of textbook writers on the criminal law including Hale and Hawkins; and (ii) *Nissan* v. *Attorney-General* (1970) where the House of Lords had to decide whether or not the Crown was liable to compensate a British subject, who owned a hotel in Cyprus, for damage done to the hotel by British forces. In reaching the conclusion that compensation was payable, the judges again examined a number of old textbooks in the attempt to discover the historical origin, and later development, of the concept of "an Act of State."

Modern textbooks

Modern textbooks are not treated as works of authority although they are frequently referred to in the courts. Counsel are permitted to adopt a textbook writer's view as part of their argument in a case. Judges will often quote from a modern textbook in the course of giving judgment; for example, in *Re Ellenborough Park* (1956) the Court of Appeal adopted the definition of an easement as defined in Cheshire's *Modern Real Property*. Sometimes the judge will decide that a statement in a textbook on a particular point is incorrect; for example, in *Watson* v. *T.S. Whitney & Co. Ltd.* (1966) the Court of Appeal decided that on a particular point both Halsbury's *Laws of England* and the High Court's *Annual Practice* were wrong.

In *R.* v. *Moloney* (1985) the House of Lords held that the definition of "intent," in Archbold's "Pleading evidence and practice in criminal cases" 40th and 41st Editions, the virtual bible of criminal court practice, was "unsatisfactory and potentially misleading."

The reason why no textbooks, since Blackstone's *Commentaries* were published in 1765, have been accepted as works of authority seems to be that (i) case reports have become fuller and much more easily accessible and (ii) by that time the principles of the common law were fully established, so that there was no question of a later textbook being itself a source of law.

One old rule which seems to have died out is the rule that a living person could not be an authority in his own lifetime. Under the present arrangements a living textbook writer can be quoted in court, and occasionally the court may refer with advantage to articles in learned law periodicals. A recent example is *Fothergill* v. *Monarch Airlines* [1980] where the House of Lords referred to a number of articles in law journals. In *Macarthys Ltd.* v. *Smith* [1981] Cumming Bruce L.J. referred in his judgment to a note by Professor Hood Phillips in the Law Quarterly Review. And in *R.* v. *Shivpuri* (1986) the House of Lords paid tribute to an article in the Cambridge Law Journal by Professor Glanville Williams. This article had a considerable influence on the court in persuading it to reverse its previous ruling.

12. Classification

1. Civil Law and Criminal Law

In the examination of the civil and criminal court structures, and the subsequent chapter on procedure, this basic division of the English legal system was observed in its practical application. The simple explanation for the division—that the state is concerned to see that misconduct, or crime, which affects the community as a whole, is punished; whilst civil law is there to provide individual members of the community with the opportunity to enforce rights, duties and obligations against other individuals—is borne out by the continuing experience of legal developments in other countries. In England the division has a long history, since it seems to be from the years following the Norman Conquest in 1066 that the first recognition of the different nature of the two branches of law took place. The royal courts came to accept what were called "pleas of the Crown," as being wrong conduct affecting the state on the one hand; and other activities involving individual wrong-doing, which the state, having provided a court and a judge, could leave to the individuals affected to settle on the other hand.

2. Criminal Law

Criminal law has long been accepted as the concern of the state. For this reason serious criminal cases are brought in the name of the Crown, and the report of the case is headed *R. v. Smith* (the name of the defendant). The letter R. represents the Latin *Rex*, or *Regina*, meaning "The King," or "The Queen." As the monarch is the fountain of justice, as well as the formal head of state, it would seem quite proper that he or she should represent the state in this context. However, in respect of many crimes any member of the public may institute criminal proceedings. Just what conduct is to be regarded as criminal is not easy to determine, since one of the characteristics of

139

criminal law is that different societies, and the same society at different times, will have varying rules about what constitutes criminal conduct. The more developed a state, the more complex its attitude to crime becomes; for example, the present-day system in this country teems with summary crimes, which are more a matter of anti-social behaviour, or even of maladministration in matters affecting the public, than deliberate wrong-doing of a serious kind. The same variety of attitudes to behaviour constituting a crime is to be found in the sanctions which are imposed as punishment for a breach of the society's code of conduct. In this country even in the course of two centuries, crimes, for which the death penalty or transportation was thought to be appropriate, may now be dealt with by a small fine or even by the defendant being put on probation. So it can be appreciated that it is necessary to examine the criminal law of a state at a particular period of time; because, although some general principles apply in that homicide and theft are inevitably crimes, there are many variations in the concept of criminal conduct which can only be discovered by detailed study. This is one reason why English tourists often make the headlines through having committed a crime abroad by conduct which is accepted here. The girl who wears a bikini in a public place, the car driver involved in an accident, the photographer taking views of the harbour, are all examples of this situation. The same variety in approach is also true of criminal punishment imposed abroad.

There are a number of ways in which crime in this country can be classified:

Summary and indictable offences

The major division of crimes is into summary and indictable offences to accord with the procedure and court structure of the English legal system. Thus, a crime will fit either into the summary or into the indictable category, and will be regarded as such from the point of view of the procedure subsequent to the arrest or charge. As differences in the form of crime have become more recognised, so this method of classification has increased in value, in that a particular form of misconduct like theft or assault or malicious damage may be tried summarily, or on indictment, depending upon the form which the crime takes and how Parliament has decided it shall be tried. The tendency is for the jurisdiction of the magistrates to be increased at the expense of trial by jury in the Crown Court. For a further consideration of criminal procedure (see p. 72).

Treason, felonies and misdemeanours

This was the accepted classification of crime in English law for a very long time, until the first section of the Criminal Law Act 1967 abolished the distinction between felonies and misdemeanours. The original distinction was based on the fact that conviction for felony automatically involved forfeiture of the offender's property; and although forfeiture was abolished by the Forfeiture Act 1870 the use of the two terms remained. The general basis was that felonies were the more serious, and misdemeanours the less serious, crimes. Treason as an offence continues to exist.

Arrestable and non-arrestable offences

To replace the distinction between felonies and misdemeanours the Criminal Law Act 1967 introduced the rather uninspired titles of arrestable and non-arrestable offences. The power of the citizen and the police officer to arrest without warrant now depends on whether or not an arrestable offence has been committed. The Act defines an arrestable offence as "any offence, or attempt to commit any offence, for which the sentence is fixed by law, or for which a person (not previously convicted) may under or by virtue of any enactment be sentenced to imprisonment for a term of five years." Other than those offences which Parliament has expressly made arrestable offences, all other such are non-arrestable offences.

A new category introduced by the Police and Criminal Evidence Act 1984 is the "serious arrestable offence."

Types of crime

Another method of classification is to take the various crimes and put them into a number of general categories. An obvious arrangement would be:

offences against the person;
offences against property; and
offences against the state.

A word of warning! The following definitions are very broad. Anyone wishing to obtain more than the vaguest overall picture of the criminal law must refer to the standard textbooks on the subject.

Offences against the person

These would include homicide in the form of murder, manslaughter, causing death by dangerous driving and infanticide; rape, indecent assault or certain other sexual offences; assault, wounding with intent to do grievous bodily harm or occasioning actual bodily harm; and bigamy. Murder can be defined as "the unlawful killing of a reasonable creature, who is in being and under the Queen's Peace, with malice aforethought, express or implied, the death fol-

lowing within a year and a day"; manslaughter has the same definition except that the words "with malice aforethought" do not
apply. Infanticide is committed when a woman by any wilful act or
omission causes the death of a child being under the age of 12
months, when suffering from the after-effects of a child birth. Rape
consists of having sexual intercourse with a woman or girl without
her consent; and bigamy is committed when any person "being married shall marry any other person during the life of the former husband or wife."

Offences against property

These will most often take the form of theft, which is now governed by the Theft Act 1968 as amended. The old term larceny has
disappeared and the term theft has taken its place. The statutory
definition of theft is: "a person is guilty of theft if he dishonestly
appropriates property belonging to another with the intention of
permanently depriving the other of it." The maximum punishment
is imprisonment for 10 years. New terminology has been introduced
whereby the former offence of obtaining by false pretences has been
renamed "obtaining property by deception," and obtaining credit
by fraud has become "obtaining a pecuniary advantage by deception." Burglary now includes house-breaking, and blackmail
replaces demanding with menaces. Finally the offence of robbery
has been retained, but the offence of receiving stolen property is now
to be known as "handling stolen goods."

Offences against the state

Not unnaturally this group of offences starts with treason, which
has always been regarded as amongst the most serious of criminal
offences. The Statute of Treason 1351 remains in force, but at the
present time prosecutions are nearly always brought under the
Official Secrets Acts' legislation. Generally this makes it an offence
to act in a way which is prejudicial to the safety or the interests of the
state. Other old offences against the Crown and the Government like
sedition seem to be obsolete. There are various offences which are
held to be against the public peace and morals, such as obscenity,
and others against public justice, like perjury. Finally some offences
in connection with trade, like coinage or currency offences, so affect
the state, that they fall into the category of being offences against the
state.

Criminal liability

In the English legal system the prosecution is required to prove
the guilt of the person accused beyond reasonable doubt. As was

seen in Chapters 7 and 8, the decision of the court as to whether or not the prosecution has succeeded is a matter for the jury where the trial is on indictment, after a trial properly conducted by the judge in accordance with established rules of procedure and evidence. In summary trials the decision is a matter for the magistrates.

In general terms no person is guilty of a criminal offence unless he has committed a guilty act—"*actus reus*"—and has a guilty mind—"*mens rea.*" The complete maxim is "*actus non facit reum nisi mens sit rea.*" Special rules apply where, for example, children, persons of unsound mind, or corporations are involved in criminal proceedings. It must also be borne in mind that Parliament can attach criminal liability to persons such as a licensee of a public-house, for an offence committed in relation to the premises or the business, where the licensee himself may be unaware of the conduct in question. An offence of this nature is called, for obvious reasons, "an absolute offence."

3. Civil Law

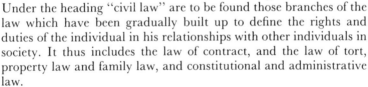

Under the heading "civil law" are to be found those branches of the law which have been gradually built up to define the rights and duties of the individual in his relationships with other individuals in society. It thus includes the law of contract, and the law of tort, property law and family law, and constitutional and administrative law.

Because all litigation in civil law is brought by one individual against another (although the "individual" may be a company or a department of state or even the mayor and corporation of a city), the case takes the form *Smith* v. *Brown*, where Smith is the surname of the plaintiff and Brown the surname of the defendant. As was seen in Chapter 5 the case, depending on its nature, is brought in one of the civil courts and separate civil procedure is followed as outlined in Chapter 7. It should perhaps be added that it is not possible from the name of the case to be sure which party is the plaintiff and which the defendant, unless one is sure that the case is one heard at first instance. Otherwise, if there has been an appeal, the appellant's name is put first and the respondent's name second, and this confuses the issue.

The same warning as regards the following brief outlines of the main subjects of the civil law which was made about the description of the main subject classifications of the criminal law (above p. 141) should be repeated here. There are many textbooks on these subjects and the student should refer to them.

Contract

One of the most important branches of civil law for which the state has to provide is that known as contract. This branch of the law deals with the enforcement of legally binding agreements entered into between parties. A contract is defined as an agreement which the law will enforce. The first problem is to discover just what distinguishes an agreement which the law will enforce, from one which the law will not enforce. In the latter category fall agreements of a social or domestic nature, where the law presumes that there never was an intention to undertake a legally binding obligation. Consequently, agreements made between a husband and wife are not, in the normal way, regarded as binding contracts. On the other hand, agreements which are entered into leading to the sale of goods, or concerning the provision of services, will be treated as expressly, or by implication, legally binding. The distinction is vital because if the agreement is a contract then the courts have extensive powers to make the parties comply with their bargain; whereas if the agreement is not a contract, then the courts have no power to assist either party.

In determining whether or not the parties have succeeded in reaching a binding agreement, there are a number of relevant factors which fall to be considered by the court. These can be summarised as: (i) offer and acceptance, (ii) intention to create legal relations, (iii) consideration, (iv) capacity, (v) genuineness of consent, (vi) legality.

By "offer and acceptance" the court requires to be satisfied that there was an offer made by one party, which was unconditionally accepted by the party to whom the offer was made. At the moment when the offer and acceptance meet, there is said to be "*consensus ad idem.*" This means that the parties have reached agreement.

The intention to create legal relations is fundamental to the whole concept of making a contract, since unless the court is satisfied that both parties, whether expressly or impliedly, have agreed that the agreement between them shall have legal consequences, it will not recognise that agreement as a contract. The person who buys a loaf of bread, or takes a short bus ride, may not consciously realise that he is, in each instance, entering into a contract; although if he discovers a piece of string in the loaf, or if the bus driver through his carelessness has an accident in which the passenger is injured, then the person concerned will take a different view of the two agreements. The courts regard such agreements as having the implied consent of the parties that they shall have legal effect, and are thus contracts.

Consideration is the value which the parties to a contract obtain under the terms of their agreement. It is the bargain which is made. The court will not examine the actual value in money terms which each party is to get, to see whether or not the exchange is reasonable; instead it will ensure that each party got what it bargained for under the agreement. The court, that is, will not set itself up as an arbiter of value; it will limit itself to seeing that the agreed consideration passed between the parties. This is what it meant by saying that "consideration must be real but need not be adequate." Another well-known term in this context is *"caveat emptor"*—let the purchaser beware. This applies because it is the purchaser of goods who makes the offer, and therefore he should take great care to ensure that he is getting the consideration he requires.

Special rules have been built up in contract to deal with the position of persons under 18—who are minors; persons who enter into contracts when drunk or suffering from mental illness; bankrupts, corporations and unincorporated associations, as to all of which see the following chapter. These rules are grouped under the heading of "capacity," in the sense that the law makes provision for the ordinary adult of sound mind, and any party who does not fall within this definition is covered by special rules.

In some circumstances the court is faced with a plea by one party that, although he has made the contract, he did not genuinely give his consent when entering into it. This may be because he made a mistake of fundamental significance to the contract, or it can be that the other party, by a misrepresentation about the subject-matter, persuaded him to make the contract. If this plea is made, the court inevitably is put on inquiry to see whether or not the contract was properly entered into. If it is found that the mistake or misrepresentation did affect the consent, the court may not allow the contract to stand.

Another factor which occasionally arises is the legality of the contract. Naturally the courts will not enforce agreements which in some substantial way infringe the law. Sometimes this occurs because Parliament specifically by legislation makes certain kinds of agreement unlawful, or it can happen because the judges decide that, as a matter of public policy, they will not give effect to certain kinds of agreement. A well-known class of contract falling within this latter category is a contract which is said to be "tainted with immorality." If the contract is found to be unlawful the court will not enforce it.

In the normal way a contract will come to an end when both parties perform the obligations which they have accepted under it. However, the courts recognise that sometimes the parties may need to be relieved of their obligations as the result of some unforeseen development which radically alters the nature of the contract. This "frustration" of contract as it is called does not occur often, and when pleaded it is not lightly accepted by the court. The final matter which needs consideration is that where an action is brought by one party against the other party to the contract alleging that there has been a breach of contract a claim is made for compensation, called damages. The general principle applied is that the award of damages should place the victim in the position he would have been in, had the contract been properly performed according to its terms.

Commercial Law

Largely based on the law of contract are a number of specialised fields of law which collectively are called commercial or mercantile law. These include such topics as agency, sale of goods, carriage of goods, credit-sale, partnership, insolvency, insurance and negotiable instruments. Whilst nearly all these topics are now governed by Acts of Parliament, they derive originally from decisions of the judges based on the customs of merchants. Hence the name "mercantile law."

Difference between a crime and a contract

Although a single set of circumstances can give rise to a criminal prosecution and an action for breach of contract, as for example the sale of the loaf of bread with the piece of string in it, this is uncommon. The majority of breaches of contract are in no way connected with the criminal law. The builder who fails to complete a house by the agreed date, or the egg supplier, who cannot comply with his contracts because his poultry are affected by fowl pest, may be in breach of contract, but they will certainly not have committed a crime.

Tort

Another important branch of civil law is that known as tort. The word "tort" comes from the medieval French and means "twisted" or "wrong." In its legal context tort is concerned with wrong conduct alleged by one individual against another individual. It will be observed that in tort the state is involved, in that it has to decide just what conduct is wrongful and what conduct is permissible, because not every kind of loss can be the subject of a successful claim. Whereas in contract the parties make the agreement, and the court is only involved to decide whether or not that agreement was properly made and then, if appropriate, to enforce it, in tort the courts have had to decide what conduct constitutes a civil wrong and to provide a remedy accordingly.

The textbooks define a tort as a breach of a duty created not by agreement, but by the law itself for the redress of which an action for damages may be brought by the injured party. Perhaps a simpler approach is to take some recognised torts and explain what factors the court will look for, in that particular form of wrong-doing. In some instances the wrong-doing may be criminal as well as civil, and in such a matter there are the two separate possible courses—prosecution by the state in respect of the crime, and an action for damages by the individual suffering personal loss.

Negligence

The most fruitful source of cases in tort is the action arising from alleged negligence. One has only to think of the claims stemming from motor-vehicle accidents, and from accidents at work, to realise that these two fields will give rise to hundreds of actions annually. Negligence occurs where, in the eyes of the law, there is a breach of a duty to take care causing loss. Of course there will be much argument about the existence of such a duty in the individual case, and about whether or not the duty has in that particular case been broken; a further factor for argument is deciding what damage is the result of the alleged negligence, and whether or not the plaintiff was guilty of contributory negligence.

Defamation

In the tort of negligence the loss caused usually takes the form either of personal injuries or of damage done to the property of the claimant, but in the tort of defamation the injury done is to personal reputation. The law holds that an individual is entitled to protection from having his reputation damaged falsely; where this has occurred, the protection is an action for libel or slander. Whereas slander is always limited to spoken defamation, libel may be written defamation, or it may be defamation in some other comparatively permanent form like television or the cinema. The tort consists in the publication of an untrue statement which tends to lower a person's reputation in the estimation of right thinking members of society. A jury will be called to try a defamation action.

Nuisance

The tort of private nuisance is committed where the conduct of one party causes substantial discomfort to another party in the enjoyment of his property. This can be a direct act as with a right of way or a right of support, but it is more likely to be conduct which, as a result of undue noise or smell or some other activity having unpleasant results, constitutes an unreasonable interference with an occupier's enjoyment of his property. In deciding what is reasonable the court will have regard to the locality and to how "the man on the Clapham omnibus" would react to the situation. If he, as the reasonable man, would find the situation intolerable the plaintiff is on sound ground; if on the other hand he would not be unduly bothered by the nuisance, the defendant will succeed.

Trespass

There are three aspects to the tort of trespass; there is the commonly recognised trespass to land, there is trespass to the person, and trespass to goods. In all three forms the essence of the matter is that it is an unjustifiable interference with the land, or the person or the goods involved. The person who uses another person's garden path as a short-cut; cases of assault, battery and unlawful arrest leading to a false imprisonment; and the theft of goods; all are cases giving rise to an action for trespass. Historically, this form of wrongful conduct was early recognised, and so the writ alleging trespass lies at the foundation of the development of the law of tort in this country.

These headings cover the most common and therefore best known types of civil wrong which the law calls tort. However it must not be overlooked that there are various other possible actions which are claims in tort, such as for conspiracy or fraud; in fact, wherever loss is caused by one party to another party, the possibility of tortious liability needs to be taken into account. In addition, there are special rules relating to the liability of children, persons of unsound mind, the Crown, and corporations which are briefly touched upon in the following chapter.

Difference between a crime and a tort

It will have been observed that one set of circumstances can be both a crime and a tort. Theft, for example, is both a criminal act against the community and a civil wrong against the individual whose property is stolen. A motor-vehicle accident may result in a prosecution for dangerous driving, as well as civil claims in negligence. In the normal way criminal proceedings are taken first, and the fact that a person has been convicted of an offence by any court in the United Kingdom shall be admissible to prove that he committed that offence. The object of the two sets of proceedings points the main practical difference. Punishment follows the conviction for crime, whereas compensation, in the form of damages to the injured party, is the result of a successful claim in tort.

Difference between a tort and a contract

The difference between tort and contract seems to lie in the fact that a contract, with its various benefits and obligations, is brought into existence by agreement of the parties. They choose whether or not to accept their respective rights and duties. In tort there is no element of choice and the parties may never have met one another; the obligations in the form of standards of conduct are imposed by the law and apply to every citizen. In the tort of negligence, for example, as Lord Atkin expressed it, there is a duty of care not to injure one's "neighbour"—"You must take reasonable care to avoid acts or omissions which you can reasonably foresee would be likely to injure your neighbour." Exactly what the standards of conduct are, and who precisely is one's "neighbour" can only be deduced by close examination of the many hundreds of cases which have actually been decided.

Family law

The change of title, introduced by the Administration of Justice Act 1970, from the Probate Divorce and Admiralty Division to the Family Division of the High Court, illustrates the now accepted importance of this subject.

Family law includes the law relating to marriage, divorce, maintenance and children; in fact all law which touches the life of the family. The law in question is now almost completely derived from legislation. For example, Parliament has specified the formalities which have to be observed for legal recognition of the status of marriage, and the powers of the courts to deal with adoption and affiliation orders, legitimation and the guardianship of infants. Special statutory provisions govern the application of the criminal law to children and young persons. A special court system has been established and a balance, between punishment and treatment to bring about reform, is carefully maintained. The emphasis is placed on the future care of the child instead of on the appropriate criminal sanctions.

An important aspect of family law is the law relating to divorce. This is now substantially contained in the Matrimonial Causes Act 1973 which substitutes the test of "irretrievable breakdown" of the marriage for the former concept of the matrimonial offence. Under the old law the party to the marriage, submitting the petition to the court asking it to dissolve the existing marriage, was obliged to show that the other party, the respondent to the petition, had committed a matrimonial offence such as adultery or cruelty. The fact that the petitioner himself or herself might also have been at fault was a secondary factor, although the petitioner was obliged to file a discretion statement where he or she had committed adultery. The present legislation treats the former matrimonial offences simply as evidence that the marriage has broken down irretrievably. The factors which point to this conclusion can be summarised as:

(i) that the respondent has committed adultery and the petitioner finds it intolerable to live with the respondent;

(ii) that the respondent has behaved in such a way that the petitioner cannot reasonably be expected to live with the respondent;

(iii) that the respondent has deserted the petitioner for a continuous period of two years;

(iv) that the parties have lived apart for two years and agree to the decree being made;

(v) that the parties have lived apart for five years.

The court retains a discretion in the making of the decree and it is required to explore the possibility of a reconciliation between the parties.

In 1985 over 190,000 petitions for divorce were filed. County courts deal with the undefended petitions whilst the High Court hears defended petitions and cases involving complex issues. Provided that there are no children of the marriage and that the petition is not to be defended it is possible for the divorce decree to be granted virtually without a hearing.

Another decree which the court can issue is a decree of nullity, declaring the marriage to be void. This decree may be available, on such grounds as failure to observe the statutory formalities required for the marriage ceremony, or physical incapacity or wilful refusal to consummate the marriage.

Constitutional and administrative law

Another branch of the civil law is concerned essentially with the individual and his relationship to the government of the state. As well as examining the various organs in the system of government from a legal standpoint, this field of law is especially concerned to define exactly where the individual stands in terms of the liberties of the subject. In a sense this is the most vital factor in all law, because however excellent and effective the law of contract or criminal law in a state may be, unless the subject has clearly defined rights to protect him against arbitrary treatment on the part of government agencies and the law enforcement bodies, then his freedom is seriously curtailed and can even be illusory.

Constitutional law is largely concerned with the existing organs of government, seeking to explain where these various bodies come from, and whence they derive their legal powers. Consequently it deals with such topics as the monarch and the royal prerogative; the functions of, and the relationship between, the House of Commons and the House of Lords; the role of the executive in the form of the Prime Minister and the Government; the structure of local government and the powers given to it; the status of the armed forces and the police; and the position of the courts and the judiciary in the constitution. Once these topics have been considered it becomes easier to appreciate the rights and duties of the citizen in the state. It is then possible to set out how far the individual enjoys freedom of the person and the right to own property, freedom of speech and the right to hold and take part in public meetings, all of which matters are included in the general term the liberties of the subject. An additional subject of growing importance is the law relating to citizenship, with particular reference to immigration.

Administrative law is a branch of the law which is becoming more important as the state plays an ever-increasing part in the affairs of the individual. Whereas originally the state's role was conceived as being limited to enforcing law and order within the state and resisting forces from without, in this century the growth of the Welfare State has caused the Government to become a very prominent factor in the lives of everyone. And the same is substantially true of local government, whose functions are now so widespread as to touch the lives of every citizen. Finally the growth of public corporations, which are often in effect state agencies, also affects the individual closely, whether in his use of public transport or in his need of fuel and light. The law which governs these various administrative agencies is of considerable practical consequence in that it closely affects the individual in the community; the most important aspect of it is the control which is exercised over the actions of these administrative authorities by the courts. Other subjects of first rank importance are delegated legislation, the making of law by subordinate authorities with Parliament's authority; proceedings involving the Crown, which term includes the civil servants employed in the central government departments of the state; and administrative tribunals and inquiries which are widely used for a variety of purposes intended to assist the state in its manifold task of administration.

The essential difference between these two branches of law would seem to be that in constitutional law the study made is of the organs as they exist, the institutions of government almost in an abstract sense, whereas administrative law is the study of those institutions actually in operation. It is clearly one thing to examine the way in which the Prime Minister and the Government establish the various government departments, but it is quite another matter to make a study of the decisions emanating from such a department, to grasp what are the decision-making methods used, and what part the law can play in controlling the work of the department and assessing the validity of the decisions taken.

Law of property

There are a number of different but important aspects to this branch of the law.

The law of property

The law of property strictly so-called, tends to concern itself with the legal theory of the ownership, occupation and use of land, defining the various elements in property law such as tenures and estates, fee simple and fee tail, and easements and profits.

Conveyancing

Conveyancing is the term given to the work of transferring the legal title in property. In the case of a sale this may well involve the purchaser obtaining a mortgage, that is, a loan of money to enable him to purchase, secured on the value of the property in question. Before the purchase can be completed, the purchaser and the mortgagee must examine the legal title to the property for the last 15 years (Law of Property Act 1969) so as to ensure that the vendor holds, and can pass, a good legal title, to the purchaser. The transfer is effected in an unregistered land area by having a conveyance properly executed and placed with the existing title deeds; where the land is registered at the Land Registry the change in ownership is effected by the execution of a transfer which leads to an amendment of the register.

Landlord and tenant

The law relating to landlord and tenant has grown very complex, to a large extent because governments have seen fit to pass legislation affecting the relationship as part of their housing policy. To lease property, instead of selling it, whereby the tenant has exclusive occupation for the fixed period on agreed terms and conditions is the basis of the law; but the legislation can affect both the agreed rent, the term of the lease, and the security of the tenant, in ways which bear little relation to the original agreement between the parties.

Succession

Inevitably death results in the need to transfer property and this forms part of the law of succession. Under this aspect of the law of property, executors or administrators are responsible for transferring property in accordance with the terms of the deceased person's will, or if no will has been left, in accordance with the statutory rules governing the distribution of the estate. Closely linked with the law of succession is the law relating to inheritance tax.

Trusts

The recognition by the court of Chancery of the legally binding nature of a trust, both on the trustees and the beneficiaries named, meant that from about the sixteenth century the trust became a characteristic feature of the law relating to property. This was particularly true of the major landowners, who took advantage of the trust to tie up their land in the interests of the family, with the result that property lawyers today need to be well acquainted with the law of trusts. In practice the trust continues to occur in property transactions more frequently than might be expected.

Terminology in the law of property
Real and personal property

Historically English law tended to develop two forms of action, real actions and personal actions, which in turn led to the designation of property as either real or personal. Real property consisted of freehold land, buildings and fixtures which could be the subject of recovery by a real action; personal property was virtually all other kinds of property, including not only personal effects, but leasehold property as well. By a quirk of history a lease was regarded in law as a simple financial investment and not as an interest in land. These definitions remain relevant in that personalty still includes leasehold interests, whilst realty is restricted to freehold land; another consequence of the distinction is that personalty can be divided into "chattels real," which are leaseholds, and "chattels personal" which consist of furniture and other personal belongings. A further division of chattels personal is into "choses in possession" and "choses in action." By "choses in possession" is meant furniture, jewellery and other personal effects, whilst "choses in action" are intangible and comprise such assets as a copyright or shares or a negotiable instrument. These may only be enforced by a legal action, which explains the title "choses in action."

Movable and immovable property

These terms are not commonly used in English law, but they do cover the layman's attitude to property, which is to divide it into personal property on the one hand and land on the other hand.

Ownership and possession

An important distinction is drawn in law between the right to possess property, as opposed to the concept of owning property. Ownership as a legal concept is far removed from the layman's approach; the law sees ownership as an aggregate of legal rights. Possession as an observable fact is a much simpler concept; there is no doubt that I possess the pullover I am wearing, but conclusively to prove my ownership of it could be very difficult.

The Law of Property Act 1925

By a number of Acts passed in 1925, of which the Law of Property Act 1925 was the most important, a thorough reform of land law was undertaken. The legislation succeeded in simplifying the existing law considerably. Now there are only two possible legal estates in land, and only five legal interests; the owner of a legal estate has complete rights over the property, whilst the owner of a legal interest has a limited right over the land. The two legal estates are a fee simple absolute in possession, meaning a freehold, and a term of years absolute, meaning a leasehold. The five legal interests are: easements and profits à prendre (rights over someone else's land); a rent charge; a charge by way of legal mortgage; a land tax or other charge imposed by law; and rights of entry over a legal rent charge. All other estates and interests take effect only in equity and as such they exist as a trust.

General

Although this chapter has concerned itself with cursory surveys of the criminal law and the most important branches of the civil law, it must not be overlooked that there are other fields of law of considerable importance which have not received a mention, but which are nonetheless of great consequence in the system. Company law, in that it deals with the law relating to the vast number of commercial corporations, which are now of such importance in the life of this country, is one such subject; the law affecting local government functions in the form of town and country planning, education, housing, highways and public health law is of great significance; the law of taxation, or revenue law, as it is sometimes called, is another branch of law of such great importance that it provides the House of Lords annually with a number of appeals. Nor has there been space to consider such matters as European Community Law, the conflict of laws, industrial law, international law, both private and public, and the law of international trade; all of which are legal subjects of immense and growing importance.

4. Private Law and Public Law

The chapter so far has concerned itself with the classification of law into its civil and criminal branches; but an alternative classification which could have been used is that into private law and public law.

Private law, on the basis of this division, includes all the branches of law which concern cases where one individual is claiming against another. It therefore takes in contract and tort and family and property law.

Public law is concerned with cases in which the state is involved, where the public has a direct interest in the result, and so includes criminal law and constitutional and administrative law. It extends to take in the law as it affects the welfare services, public corporations and the many functions of local government.

5. Common Law and Equity

Another approach to the topic is to classify English law on the basis of its historical development, and this produces a division between those fields of law which were the concern of the Common Law, and those which derived from Equity. Chapter 14, as an outline historical survey of the subject, will explain this classification at greater length.

6. Substantive Law and Adjective Law

It is possible to divide law into what is called substantive law, being the legal principles established by the courts in a particular branch of the law, and adjective law, which is concerned only with the procedure used in those courts. In a complex legal system, such as the English system, there develop very detailed rules making up adjective law, as is evidenced by the Rules of the Supreme Court and the County Court Rules.

7. Common Law and Statute Law

Another classification, which is referred to in Chapter 14 at p. 173, is into common law, that is, law based upon judicial precedents, and statute law, which is law laid down by Act of Parliament or by a Statutory Instrument made under an Act of Parliament. These terms are explained in Chapter 11, above, in the sections on Legislation and Case Law.

8. Civil Law and Common Law

The English legal system, and the systems deriving from it, are often spoken of as common law systems. Such a system is based on the continuous legal history of this country with considerable stress laid on precedent and the interpretation of statutes. On the continent, however, most legal systems are based on codes of law which can be traced back to Roman law. These systems are known as Civil Law systems.

9. Civil Law and Ecclesiastical Law

This distinction is obvious: civil law is law relating to non-religious matters, ecclesiastical law relates to religious matters. This distinction was considerably more important in earlier times than it is now, because such matters as probate and divorce fell to the ecclesiastical courts until the mid-nineteenth century. See below, p. 178.

10. Civil Law and Military Law

This distinction also is obvious; civil law in this sense is non-military law; military law is concerned with the discipline of the armed forces of the Crown. As has been seen (at p. 63, above) military law is enforced in courts martial in accordance with statutory authority.

13. Legal Personality

1. Legal Recognition

Whereas in everyday speech the word "person" is used to describe an individual human being, in law a legal person may be an individual human being, or it may be, for example, a group of individuals which the law recognises as having a legal personality of its own. Legal personality involves the acceptance of those rights and obligations which are recognised and given effect by the law. Different legal systems have taken varying views of legal personality; in some states idols, relics of saints and certain animals have been regarded as legal persons, whereas slaves and outlaws have at times had no standing in law, being without legal personality.

In the English legal system at the present time the main division is into "natural" legal persons, *i.e.* human beings, and "artificial" legal persons, *i.e.* a group of human beings recognised as having its own existence in law. Natural legal persons inevitably form the largest group and all branches of law are designed to deal with the conduct or misconduct of such individuals. One thinks of the criminal law, the law relating to property, and the law of tort as examples of legal rules being established to meet the human situation. Inevitably the law is built up on the assumption that it has to deal with the normal human adult of full mental and physical capacity. A consideration of the exceptions to this assumption, for example, children and young persons, persons of unsound mind, and persons drunk or under drugs, will be necessary. A detailed examination of the artificial legal persons, which are recognised as having legal personality, is also called for, and will form the final section of this chapter.

2. Natural Legal Persons

Special legal rules have to be applied to the human individual who is not an adult of full age and capacity.

Children and young persons

The age of majority is now 18 (Family Law Reform Act 1969). In law a person below the age of 18 is a minor, or infant, and special rules of law apply.

Criminal offences by persons under the age of 17 are tried in specially constituted courts, called juvenile courts. The magistrates are specially selected and of the three who form the court there must be at least one woman. The hearing is not open to the public but the press can be present and can report the circumstances of the offence, but not particulars which would cause the child or young person concerned to be identified. In exceptional circumstances the magistrates can permit the disclosure of identity but this is very rare. If a child, defined as being between the ages of 10 and 14, or a young person, 14 to 17, is convicted of a criminal offence, this is known as a finding of guilt, so as to distinguish it from the recorded convictions of an adult. A child under the age of 10 is not deemed to be capable of criminal intent; in due course it is proposed to raise this age to 12 and ultimately to 14.

In terms of punishment it is the practice not to send a child or young person to prison. Age is obviously a mitigating factor and the court in deciding on punishment takes account of the full circumstances of the child or young person before pronouncing sentence.

Legislation which has yet to be brought into force attempts to introduce a different approach to the problem. For children and young persons "care" proceedings in the juvenile court will take the place of criminal proceedings, and this may result in a "care order" being made in the interests of the child. The principle which will be applied is to be "care" rather than "punishment." An exception retaining criminal proceedings is made for alleged homicide.

In contract the presumption is made that a person under 18, who may be known as either an "infant" or a "minor" in this context, should be protected against his own commercial inexperience. To this end the courts have consistently refused to regard contracts entered into by an infant as binding upon him; the two exceptions to this rule, where the courts are prepared to regard the contracts as binding, are first, a contract for "necessaries" and second, a contract of an educational or training nature, which is "for the infant's benefit." The term "necessaries" includes clothing, food and other goods "suitable to the condition in life of the infant and to his actual requirements at the time of sale and delivery"; even where such a contract is valid it is laid down that the infant is only liable to pay a reasonable price for the "necessaries."

The majority of contracts made by an infant are voidable at the choice of the infant; this means that the infant can escape from such a contract if he chooses to do so, although he cannot, it seems, recover back money which he has paid under the contract. Under an Act of Parliament, the Infants' Relief Act 1874, there are three types of contract which if made by an infant cannot be given effect. These are a contract for money lent or to be lent, a contract for the sale of goods other have necessaries, and an account stated. (This last-named category describes a series of complicated cross-accounts in which it is agreed that items on both sides should be set against each other and only the balance paid.) The statute states that all such contracts listed in the Act are to be treated as absolutely void.

This attempt to protect an infant has not always turned out to his advantage, particularly when the age of majority was 21, and thous-ands of "infants" were marrying and having children, and yet in theory were not able to bind themselves in contract. Perhaps the big-gest handicap was their inability to arrange a mortgage to finance their home buying. These difficulties are no longer so pertinent with the change in the age of majority, but the law continues in this branch to make no allowance for the arbitrary dividing line between infancy and adult status.

In the law of tort the law does not provide anything like the same protection for infants as it does in contract. In fact the general rule is that an infant is liable for the torts which he commits and must therefore pay damages, as an adult would have to in similar circum-stances. The courts mitigate the apparent severity of this rule by a common sense approach on the basis that one cannot expect the same standard of care and awareness in a child or young person, that one has a right to expect in an adult. Age is thus a vital con-sideration.

Parents are not, as a general principle, liable for the torts commit-ted by their children, but an exception can be made if the parent is, as a result of his own negligence, partly responsible for the tort com-mitted. The father, who allowed his 15-year-old son to continue using an air gun, although he knew that his son was using it irres-ponsibly, was liable for the injury to another child resulting from his son's misuse of the gun: *Bebee* v. *Sales* (1916).

Persons of unsound mind

The law, inevitably, has to make provision for adults who are of unsound mind. In criminal law the difficulty is to ascertain precisely the dividing line between sanity and insanity. The courts established a guide in the M'Naghten Rules (1843) which laid down that to suc-ceed in a plea of insanity the accused must show either that he did not appreciate the nature and quality of his act, or that he did not know that what he was doing was wrong. In response to criticism of these rules a defence of "diminished responsibility" was introduced by the Homicide Act 1957. This defence applies to reduce a murder charge to manslaughter, and it defines diminished responsibility as such abnormality of mind as substantially impairs the accused's mental responsibility for his acts or omissions. An example of the problem was *R. v. Sutcliffe* [1981]—the Yorkshire Ripper Case. If the accused is found to be insane, the court's finding is that he is "not guilty by reason of insanity," and he is thereafter detained in a mental hospital.

A person of unsound mind, who enters into a contract, will be held bound to the contract unless it can be shown that the other party to the contract knew of his insanity. In tort there are few cases as a guide but it would seem, as a general principle, that persons of unsound mind are liable for the torts which they commit.

The High Court, on behalf of the Lord Chancellor, has substantial powers of management over the estates of such persons, and under the Mental Health Act 1983 the Court of Protection within the Chancery Division plays a substantial part in handling the affairs of these unfortunate individuals.

While both infants and persons of unsound mind are legal persons in that they may both bring actions in civil matters in the courts and be sued in many cases, it is nonetheless true that they have a different status in the courts in that they must both sue by a next friend and defend by a guardian *ad litem*.

Drunkenness

The law in contract and tort takes a somewhat similar view of drunkenness to that which it does of insanity. However in criminal law matters there are offences where drunkenness, far from excusing guilt, is either a constituent element in the offence or can make the commission of the offence more serious. The same is true in general of a person acting under the influence of drugs. For an example of the House of Lords having to examine self-induced intoxication as a defence to a criminal charge see *D.P.P. v. Majewski* [1976].

A person serving a term of imprisonment

Such a person is deprived of certain rights whilst serving his term of imprisonment and possibly for a period of time thereafter. This applies to such matters as the right to vote, jury service and candidature for parliamentary and local elections.

Bankruptcy

A man who is made bankrupt loses the right to handle his own affairs; it is as if his apparent financial incapacity causes him to forfeit this right. The trustee in bankruptcy takes over the debtor's affairs and endeavours to administer them for the creditors' benefit. A bankrupt must not make contracts without disclosing that he is an undischarged bankrupt; if he does so he commits a criminal offence.

Married women

A married woman now has complete independence in law to bind herself by contract, to make herself liable in tort and to answer for her crimes. This state of affairs is comparatively recent; it is only since 1935 that a husband has not been liable for the torts of his wife, and only since 1962 that a husband could sue his wife and vice versa.

Aliens

A person, who is not a British subject nor a British protected person, is known as an alien whilst in this country. He is subject to the ordinary criminal law, is liable on his torts and is generally free to enter into contracts. One long-standing restriction on this freedom is that he cannot make a contract to buy shares in a British ship. Naturally an alien does not have the power to vote in parliamentary or municipal elections, or to be a candidate in local or parliamentary elections. Under legislative enactments he cannot work in the United Kingdom unless he has a work permit. Special provisions apply to visitors from the European Community.

Nationality

One of the fundamental matters which concerns any legal system is the decision as to who are to be regarded as citizens, to whom it laws will expressly apply, and who are not. The privilege of citizenship clearly involves both rights and obligations; and the definition of citizenship is a part of the law regarding nationality. Persons who do not so qualify are called aliens.

The general rules concerning nationality in this country are, at present, contained in the British Nationality Act 1981 as amended; but the position has been complicated by the very close connections which have existed between this country and the Commonwealth. In particular, the Immigration Act 1971 has drawn a distinction between United Kingdom citizens having a right to reside in the United Kingdom and those technically possessing citizenship but having no right to reside. The result is that those in the latter category may only take up residence in the United Kingdom subject to strict conditions.

Domicile

The former law on the subject of domicile has been changed by the Civil Jurisdiction and Judgments Act 1982. In order to bring us into line with our European brethren it is now laid down that a person is domiciled where he is resident and where he has a substantial connection.

The Crown

This term has a number of different meanings all of which stem from the constitutional history of England and Wales. When used of the monarch as the formal head of state the well-known maxim that "the Crown can do no wrong" applies. The monarch thus retains a specially privileged position in law in that no provisions exist for bringing an action against her. The logic of this is that as the courts are the Queen's Courts, and as the judges are Her Majesty's judges, there is no court or judge able to try a case in which she is directly involved.

For a long time servants of the Crown were able to hide behind this immunity of the Crown from legal process, so that until the Crown Proceedings Act 1947 the only possible remedy for misconduct on the part of a Crown servant was by a petition of right seeking compensation on an *ex gratia* basis. The 1947 Act in general terms makes the Crown as an institution, and therefore its servants, capable of being sued in contract and in tort like an ordinary individual with only a few reservations. Exceptions were made for the Post Office, now restated in the Post Office Act 1969, and for the armed services of the Crown. Nonetheless, the result is that now, in the English legal system, it is possible to have a government department as defendant to an action in the ordinary courts, in much the same way as one can have an individual as defendant.

3. Artificial Legal Persons

Corporations and unincorporated associations

The word "artificial" is not perhaps the happiest choice to describe these legal persons, but it does point to the significant factor that, in contrast to the previous categories, these legal persons are recognised, subject to certain conditions, as having an independent status in law although they have no human characteristics.

The word used to describe these artificial legal persons is "corporations." For several centuries the courts in the English legal system have been prepared to recognise the existence of such corporations in the sense that they have attributed legal personality to them. When a corporation is deemed to come into existence is a matter for the courts to decide, so that it is not every group activity which results in the establishment of a corporation. Bodies, which are not so recognised, are generally known as "unincorporated associations."

The most prominent examples of corporations are limited liability companies, local authorities and public corporations. All of these make a major contribution to the living standards of the modern state and inevitably feature largely in modern law. This can be seen in that the largest contracts made today are almost always made between corporations, rather than between individuals; in the law of tort corporations frequently appear as defendants and sometimes as plaintiffs. Only in criminal law is the corporation of less significance and even here successful prosecutions are sometimes brought against a corporation for a technical offence committed by its agents.

Corporations

Creation. The courts accept that a corporation can be brought into existence either by the monarch, through the exercise of the ancient royal prerogative power to grant a royal charter, or by Parliament, exercising its undoubted supremacy to bestow corporate personality by passing an Act to that effect.

Although the royal power to grant charters of incorporation remains, the firmly established convention that the monarch will act in this matter only on the advice of the government of the day means that in practice the power is not frequently used. Once in a while some learned profession will be incorporated by royal charter, like the Royal Institute of British Architects; or in the same way a new municipal corporation will be granted corporate status, or a new university will be brought into existence and its powers defined. In the exercise of this function the monarch acts on the advice of a committee of the Privy Council, which engages in full consultation with interested government departments. The state has come a long way from the time when the monarch's grant of a royal charter depended entirely on his own discretion and was normally conditioned by commercial considerations. For several centuries the boroughs were in the habit of negotiating terms with the monarch whereby, in return for a cash settlement, special privileges were confirmed or granted to the borough in question. The same considerations applied to the grant of charters to trading bodies and to monopolies.

The power of Parliament by legislation to create new corporations takes two forms; direct creation and indirect creation.

1. An Act may specifically establish a corporation, as when a public corporation is brought into existence, for example the Coal Industry Nationalisation Act 1946, which established the National

Coal Board and spelled out its functions. Another example is the county and district council set up by the Local Government Act 1972 where section 2(3) of the Act expressly states that each such council "shall be a body corporate."

2. The second method of creation is for Parliament to pass an Act under which, if a certain procedure is observed, the resulting body is to be recognised as a corporation. The most important example is the legislation leading to the creation of the commercial corporations known as limited liability companies. Under successive Companies Acts, the latest legislation being the Companies Act 1985, a group of individuals can by filing the necessary documents with the Registrar of Companies and paying the fees laid down, form themselves into a company for trading purposes. The formation of such a company is thus through indirect creation by Act of Parliament.

Classification. There are several terms which are used to distinguish between corporations. As has been seen above there are two methods of creation and consequently on this basis there are "statutory corporations," those created by Parliament, and "charter corporations," those created under the royal prerogative.

Another classification is into those corporations which are made up of a number of individuals, the shareholders of a company, or the chairman and councillors of a local authority, which corporations are known as "corporations aggregate"; and in contrast, those corporations, which are made up of one person holding a public office, like the Queen or the Bishop of Durham, where the public office is called a "corporation sole."

Characteristics. Once a corporation has its separate legal personality recognised by the law, it has, so far as that is possible, the same rights and duties as all other legal persons. It can thus sue and be sued in contract, tort and property law and may even be the defendant in criminal proceedings.

One very real advantage which a corporation has is the fact that it never dies; it thus enjoys what the law calls "perpetual succession." This is obvious in the case of the shares in a company and in the composition of the council of a local authority, but it is perhaps less apparent in the case of a corporation sole. The law takes the view that when the human occupant of the office dies, the public office continues to exist and a new appointment will take it over forthwith. This is made particularly evident on the death of a reigning monarch when the first action after the announcement of the death is the proclamation of the new monarch. Hence the cry, "The King is dead; Long Live the King." The same reasoning explains why a bishop always signs documents with his own Christian name followed by the title of his diocese; when he dies there will simply be a change in the human individual occupying the office and probably a change of Christian name—but the public office will remain unaffected by the inevitable change of occupant.

As well as having this characteristic of perpetual succession a corporation also has a common seal which is used to authenticate the decisions of the corporation. At one time the use of its common seal was essential to a corporation in entering into contracts, but the inconvenience of this formality led to the common law relaxing the requirement for cases of trifling importance, or frequent occurrence, or where necessity demanded. Later Parliament recognised the need for change so that companies, and all other corporations, under the Corporate Bodies Contracts Act 1960, have been given wide powers to make contracts in the same way as other legal persons. Nonetheless for contracts of importance the common seal of a corporation continues to be used.

In the case of a statutory corporation the powers which it has are defined by the legislation which creates and governs it, and if it purports to exercise a function in excess of those powers, it is said to act "*ultra vires.*" This doctrine of *ultra vires* applies to companies as well as to local authorities and public corporations. Any such action is unlawful and the courts will not give effect to it. In the case of a local authority the councillors themselves may by order of the High Court be required to refund *ultra vires* expenditure to the rate fund. There is little doubt that the doctrine of *ultra vires* does not apply to royal charter corporations. The theory is that if such a corporation acts in contravention of its charter, the remedy is for the monarch to forfeit the charter. This apparent advantage of the charter corporation is of less value in practice because generally Parliament has enacted statutory provisions, which must be observed by all corporations affected, irrespective of their mode of creation. There is a well established principle that where a statutory provision and a prerogative power conflict, the statutory power must prevail.

So far as the individuals who make up the human element of a corporation aggregate, the shareholders and councillors, are concerned, the fact that the corporation has separate legal personality means that they have no personal responsibility for the debts incurred by the corporation. This is one reason for forming a company; because once the shareholder has accepted the obligation to pay for his shares, his financial responsibility is limited to that obligation. This explains the formal title of the "limited liability" company. No creditor of a corporation can look to individuals to pay the money owed, his remedy lies against the corporation and its assets. It follows that if a corporation gets seriously into debt it can be wound up, or put into liquidation, just as an individual can be made bankrupt.

In the same way a corporation whose function is complete can be brought to an end. In some instances it may be necessary for Parliament to pass an Act to terminate the existence of a corporation, for example the Local Government Act 1985 abolished the Greater London Council and the metropolitan county councils, but so far as companies are concerned the existing legislation provides for the winding up of a company, if the shareholders decide that this is necessary or desirable, or if the unpaid creditors take the appropriate legal action.

Unincorporated association

These are groups of individuals forming a collective association which has not obtained corporate status. The most prominent examples are partnerships and social clubs. Consequently, as the body has no separate legal personality, the individual members of it remain liable for the debts of the association. By the rules of the association it may be that particular officers of it are personally liable for their actions, but this is a matter between the individual officer and the members.

A partnership is governed by the Partnership Act 1890, and although it is an unincorporated association a legal provision allows partners to sue and be sued in their firm name. It is usual to contrast partnerships with the corporate status of a limited liability company. The main differences between these two forms of commercial activity can be summarised as:

Creation. The company is brought into being under the formalities laid down in the Companies Act 1985; a partnership is a straightforward matter of agreement between the partners.

Legal status. The company has its own legal personality; it has corporate status, perpetual succession and a common seal. A partnership has no separate legal personality.

Number. A company must have a minimum of two shareholders but there is no fixed maximum number of shareholders. A partnership may not have more than 20 members unless it involves solicitors, accountants, members of a stock exchange or certain other professions.

Financial liability. Shareholders are not personally liable for the debts incurred by the company. A creditor can proceed only against the assets of the company. In a partnership the partners are individually answerable for the debts incurred by any one of the partners in the course of the partnership business.

Powers. The company is limited by its Articles and Memorandum of Association. If it exceeds its powers the doctrine of *ultra vires* applies and generally the activity is unlawful and of no legal effect. In a partnership the powers of the partners are flexible and can be altered by mutual agreement.

Public knowledge. The Articles and Memorandum of Association of the company and also its accounts are available for inspection by any interested member of the public. The partnership arrangements are private to the members of the partnership.

Agency. Shareholders of a company are not able to bind the company by their actions, since authority is vested in the Board of Directors. All partners have implied authority to bind the partnership, provided the contracts are usual to the firm's business.

Transfer of interest. Shares in a company are generally transferable to anyone without the consent of other members unless the Articles provide otherwise. In a partnership a partner cannot transfer his interest to a third party without the consent of the other partners.

4. Trade unions

The importance of trade unions in modern society is such that specific legislation has been enacted to deal with the legal recognition of these institutions, their powers and responsibilities and, not least in importance, their immunity from certain legal obligations. The major legislation in force is the Trade Union and Labour Relations Acts 1974 and 1976 as amended by the Employment Acts 1980 and 1982 and the Trade Unions Act 1984.

14. History

1. Continuity

In the foregoing chapters a survey has been attempted of the various elements in the English legal system as it exists in 1986. It is now necessary to complete the picture, for an examination to be made in outline of the history of the system so that the emergence of the present structure can be fully appreciated. The most pertinent factor of this study is that the history is a continuing one; the British system of government, and the legal institutions which form part of it, is only explicable in terms of history. The Inns of Court, the Queen's Bench and Chancery Divisions of the High Court, the justice of the peace and the jury—these institutions, like many in the system all have a long history.

One important factor is that whereas most continental legal systems rely heavily on legal principles derived from Roman Law, the English legal system has remained comparatively uninfluenced by this source. The reasons for this would seem to be connected with the unbroken historical development of the system in England, where at no time was it felt necessary to look outside the principles of Common Law or Equity for assistance. Inevitably, through the ecclesiastical courts in particular, some Roman Law influence can be traced, but in general terms this is very limited, and especially when comparison is made with systems elsewhere.

2. Early History

Anglo-Saxon laws

The earliest English laws of which there is documentary evidence date from the Anglo-Saxon period of English history before the Norman Conquest. These laws are not strictly English laws; more accurately they are the laws relating to a particular tribal area such as Kent, Wessex or Mercia. In practice these laws are based on what seems to have been the original customs of the settlers in question. Not unnaturally there are marked discrepancies in the details of the laws remaining from the different areas. They clearly derive from the time before England emerged as a national unit.

The Norman Conquest (1066)

The Anglo-Saxon divisions were just giving way to a national entity when the Norman invasion of England occurred. The result of the Battle of Hastings in 1066 led to William the Conqueror ascending the English throne determined on a process of centralisation. William's tactics were to impose strong national government and this he did by causing his Norman followers to become the major land-owners throughout the country. The system used was "subin-feudation" under which all land belonged to the monarch and was by him granted to his followers on certain conditions. In turn they could grant their land to their tenants, again subject to conditions, those tenants could make similar grants, and so on down the ladder. This method of granting land created the complete feudal system under which tenants owed duties to their lord, whilst he in turn owed duties to his lord and so on up to the monarch, as the supreme point of the feudal pyramid. However, the system never became as firmly entrenched in this country as it did, for instance, in France.

Feudal courts

In the development of the feudal system a characteristic benefit to the feudal lord was the right to hold his own court. From the holding of this court he would obtain financial benefits, whilst at the same time it gave him very effective power over the locality. So far as the ordinary individual was concerned this local manor court was the one which affected him most. Bearing in mind that the concept of central authority in law and government was still comparatively new, it was to take a long time before the royal courts were able to exercise control over these local courts. Although the passage of centuries did see the transfer of real power from local to national courts, these feudal courts remained in being in many instances down to the property law legislation of 1925. Until 1925 there was a tenure of property called "copyhold," which involved the registration of the transaction in the local court roll so that the person held the land by "copy" of the court roll. This was a survival of a feudal court responsibility.

Royal courts

Following the Norman Conquest, succeeding monarchs soon realised that besides the need for strong national government there was also a need for the development of a system of national law and order. To this end the closest advisers of the monarch—the *"curia regis,"* or "King's council," as it was called—encouraged, over a period of time, the establishment of three separate royal courts which sat at Westminster. These were:

(i) the Court of Exchequer, which as the name implies was mainly concerned with cases affecting the royal revenue, but which also had a limited civil jurisdiction;

(ii) the Court of King's Bench, which taking its name from the original concept of the monarch sitting with his judges *"in banco"*—on the bench—at Westminster, dealt with both civil and criminal cases in which the King had an interest; and

(iii) the Court of Common Pleas, which was established to hear civil cases brought by one individual against another.

Each of the courts had its own judges. In the Court of Exchequer sat judges called Barons, with a presiding judge known as the Chief Baron. This court appears to be the oldest of the three, emerging in recognisable form in the early thirteenth century having developed out of the financial organisation responsible for the royal revenues. The Court of King's Bench had its own Chief Justice and separate judges, and was closely linked with the monarch and the Great Council for a very long time. This was due, in particular, to the original understanding that this was the court which followed the King's person. The Court of Common Pleas had its own Chief Justice and judges and left records from the early thirteenth century.

All three courts seem to have been required by the monarch— Stow in his survey of London says in 1224—to make their base in Westminster Hall and there arose continuing conflicts between them over jurisdiction. The importance of getting more and more work was largely brought about by the fact that the judges were paid out of the court fees. At any rate these three royal courts, later added to by the introduction of a Court of Chancery, survived five centuries before being reconstructed into the present High Court of Justice in the Judicature Acts 1873–1875. The ultimate merger of Exchequer and Common Pleas into the Queen's Bench Division came about in 1880.

3. The Common Law

Origin

As a centralised system of law and order gradually developed, so it became necessary for the various customary laws of the different regions to give way to national laws. This national law came to be known as the Common Law. It was called "Common" because it was common to the whole country, as opposed to the local customs which had previously predominated in the different regions. Since inevitably the different customs at times turned out to be in conflict, the decisions of the judges, absorbing certain of these customs and rejecting others, came to be of first-rate importance. They were creating "the law of the realm." Consequently, a vital feature of the original establishment of the Common Law is that it is derived entirely from case law.

Development

The Norman Kings, in attempting to weld the country together, made use of royal commissioners to travel the country to deal with governmental matters of one kind and another. The production of the "Domesday Book," as a property and financial survey, is the best known example of this system. The extension of these activities to the judicial field seems to have arisen not long after the Conquest, when the King would appoint judges as royal commissioners, charged with certain royal powers, to travel different parts of the country to deal with civil and criminal matters in the locality in which they arose.

The sending of judges, or, as they were originally called, "itinerant justices in Eyre," around the country, dates from not long after the Conquest; but the assize system, as later developed, really dates from the reign of Henry II (1154–89). The assize system only came to an end with the passing of the Courts Act 1971.

It was an important part of the work of these judges to formulate the Common Law. A task which over a lengthy period of time they did, by meeting together formally and informally to resolve problems which had arisen in the cases coming before them. The principles of law thus laid down, once accepted and developed, formed the Common Law. As these judges were linked with the courts meeting in Westminster Hall, the building up of a national system grew apace. However, the Common Law never completely abolished local custom. In fact, as we have seen in the chapter on Sources, custom has remained a source of law to the present time, even though it rarely applies today.

Forms of action

In addition to settling principles of law which were to be followed nationally, the courts also began to establish formal rules relating to the procedure to be adopted in cases coming before them. These rules laid down early that actions were to be begun by the issue of a royal writ, and that the claim made was to be set out in an accepted fashion. This was called a form of action and over a period of time the system took on rigidity in that the judges came to take the view that unless a claimant could find an appropriate form of action his claim was not one known to the law. The court officials responsible for the issue of writs tried initially to satisfy the demands of claimants by drawing up a new form of action, but the judges frowned on this course and the practice was stopped by the Provisions of Oxford 1258. So great was the resulting dissatisfaction that 30 years later by the Statute of Westminster 1285 this strict approach was slightly relaxed, so that the officials could issue a new writ, where the new situation was closely related to that covered by an existing writ. The new writs so issued became known as writs *"in consimili casu."* The effect which the writ system had on the development of the legal system is seen below in the section concerning Equity.

Common law remains in being today in that the decisions of judges are still adding to it and in theory the legislation produced by Parliament is supplementing it. Every development in the system operates on the basis that its foundation is the Common Law. Some confusion has arisen because there are several different meanings attaching to the term:

(i) In the historical sense which has already been examined. Common Law refers to the national law of this country as opposed to local law or custom. It is the law "common" to England and Wales.

(ii) Sometimes the term is used to mean the law as made by the judges, in contrast to the law as made by Parliament. In this context Common Law is limited to case decisions or precedents coming from the Courts of Common Law and Equity; and so does not include legislation. It must not be overlooked that as a result of the doctrine of parliamentary supremacy legislation can always change or overrule the Common Law.

(iii) As the next section will show, there were, for centuries in England and Wales, two parallel systems of law, one known as the Common Law and the other as Equity. In some contexts the term Common Law does not include the law derived from the Courts of Equity.

(iv) Finally the term Common Law may be used to draw a contrast to systems of foreign law. Here Common Law takes in both Equity and Legislation in that it means the complete law of England and Wales. When referring to an overseas country which has derived its legal system from England and

Wales the term Common Law system or jurisdiction is used.
This explains why sometimes an English judge will find case
decisions from such countries helpful in his consideration of a
case.

4. Equity

Origin
The difficulty which was experienced in the Common Law courts
in relation to the use of writs and the forms of action led to increasing dissatisfaction with the system. Litigants who were unable to get
satisfaction from the courts turned to the monarch and petitioned
him to do justice to his subjects and provide them with a remedy.
The monarch handed these petitions on to the Lord High Chancellor, who, as Keeper of the King's Conscience and an ecclesiastic,
seemed to be a suitable person to deal with them. He set up his own
Court of Chancery where he, or his representative, would sit to dispose of these petitions. In doing this work the Lord Chancellor
would be guided by equity, or fairness, in coming to his decisions,
Consequently, the legal decisions which succeeding Lord Chancellors made came to be known collectively as Equity. The system
seems to have become well established in the course of the fifteenth
century.

Because of the rapid increase in the judicial nature of the work, it
was soon found necessary to have a lawyer as Lord Chancellor. The
discretion vested in early Lord Chancellors gradually gave way to a
system of judicial precedent in Equity, but it was a long time before
the Common Law joke, about equity being long or short like the
Chancellor's foot, died. In practice both Common Law and Equity
came to operate as parallel systems, with each set of courts regarding itself as bound by its own judicial precedents.

Development
Having once begun to remedy the wrongs brought about by the
rigidity and technicality of the Common Law system, Equity soon
found itself establishing a jurisdiction over matters where the Common Law had failed, and continued to fail, to recognise legal rights
and duties. The law relating to trusts, for example, was entirely
based on decisions of the Court of Chancery. Nonetheless Equity
was always a "gloss" on the Common Law; it always presumed the
existence of the Common Law and simply supplemented it where
necessary. That it continued to exist for some five centuries is an
indication of the unchanging nature of English legal institutions, as

well as of the important contribution which equity made to the development of English law.

(a) Examples of new rights. The whole of the law of trusts, which was to become an important aspect of property law owed its existence entirely to the willingness of Equity to recognise and enforce the obligation of a trustee to a beneficiary.

Equity accepted the use of the mortgage as a method of borrowing money against the security of real property, when the Common Law took a literal view of the obligation undertaken by the borrower. It introduced the "equity of redemption" to enable a borrower to retain the property which was the security for the loan, even where there was default under the strict terms of the mortgage deed.

(b) Examples of new remedies. At Common Law the only remedy for breach of contract was damages, a money payment as compensation for the loss suffered. Equity realised that in some cases damages was not an adequate remedy, and therefore proceeded to introduce the equitable remedies of injunction and specific performance. An injunction is used to prevent a party from acting in breach of his legal obligations; a decree of specific performance is used to order a party to carry out his side of a contract. These remedies mean that a party to a contract cannot just decide to break it and pay damages.

Other equitable remedies are the declaratory order or judgment; the right to have a deed corrected by the process known as rectification; and the right to rescind (withdraw from) a contract. The willingness of Equity to intervene where fraud was proved, and its preparedness to deal with detailed accounts in the law of trusts and the administration of estates, also gained it wide jurisdiction. The appointment of a receiver is another solution to the problem of the management of certain financial matters, and was introduced by Equity.

(c) Examples of new procedures. In contrast to the Common Law attitudes Equity favoured a flexibility of approach. Consequently it was prepared, by a "subpoena," to order witnesses to attend, to have them examined and cross-examined orally, to require relevant documents to be produced, known as Discovery of Documents, to insist on relevant questions being answered, by the use of Interrogatories, and to have the case heard in English, where the Common Law for centuries used Latin. In the event of a failure to comply with an order, Equity was prepared to impose immediate sanctions for this contempt of court.

Another classification sometimes employed is to define the jurisdiction of Equity as exclusive, concurrent and auxiliary. In the exclusive jurisdiction sense, Equity recognised actions, as in trusts and mortgages, where the Common Law would provide no remedy; in the concurrent jurisdiction sense Equity would add to the remedies provided by the Common Law, as by the introduction of the injunction and the decree of specific performance; in the auxiliary jurisdiction sense Equity employed a more flexible procedure than the Common Law. It will be seen that these three terms simply emphasise the ways in which Equity can be seen to be related to, but to be different from, Common Law.

Maxims of Equity

As a result of its supplemental role, it became possible over the years for an observer to point to certain characteristics of Equity. These became so well known as to be called the maxims of Equity. Among the most famous are:

He who comes to Equity must come with clean hands;
Equity will not suffer a wrong to be without remedy;
Delay defeats Equity; and
Equity looks to the intent rather than to the form.

The maxims emphasise that Equity, being based in its origins on fairness and natural justice, attempted to maintain this approach throughout its later history. Certainly the judges retained their personal discretion, so that equitable remedies were not, and are not, obtainable as of right.

Relationship between Common Law and Equity

Early history. Naturally, as might be presumed, in the early stages of their respective development relations between the two systems were comparatively strained. The Common Law lawyers regarded Equity as an interloper, lacking the firmly-based legal principles with which they were familiar. They were unable, unlike the modern observer with the advantage of hindsight, to see that Equity was invaluable in remedying deficiencies in the Common Law and in encouraging the latter to develop its substantive law and procedure.

As the Court of Chancery built up its jurisdiction and the two systems could be seen to be operating on a parallel basis, inevitably the question arose, what was to happen in the unusual instance when there was a conflict? This problem was solved by James I, in the *Earl of Oxford's* case (1615), by a ruling that where there was such a conflict the rules of Equity were to prevail.

The later history of Equity was dogged in the eighteenth and nineteenth centuries by the Courts of Chancery becoming overburdened with work, with increasing reliance being placed on judicial precedent and consequent delays. Dickens' attack in his novel, *Bleak House*, on the delays and costs in the system, seems to have been thoroughly justified, with some examples of cases awaiting judgment dragging on for scores of years until both parties were dead. Parliament in the 1850s endeavoured by legislation—the Common Law Procedure Acts 1852–1854 and the Chancery (Amendment) Act 1858—to ease the position, but the dual systems continued in being, to the sometimes substantial detriment of litigants, until the Judicature Acts 1873–1875.

5. Nineteenth Century Developments

The Supreme Court of Judicature Acts 1873–1875

This legislation reorganised the existing court structures completely, and in the process formally brought together the Common Law courts and the Courts of Chancery. In the Supreme Court of Judicature set up by the Acts, the three original royal courts became three Divisions of the new High Court of Justice, the Court of Chancery which administered Equity became the fourth Division, *i.e.* the Chancery Division of the High Court, and a fifth Division, dealing with those matters not within Common Law or Equity, namely Probate, Divorce and Admiralty, completed the new arrangement. By Order in Council in 1880 the three royal courts were merged to form the Queen's Bench Division, thus leaving the three Divisions of the High Court—Queen Bench, Chancery and Probate, Divorce and Admiralty—which were then to remain unchanged for 90 years.

The Judicature Acts 1873–1875 placed on a statutory basis the old rule that where Common Law and Equity conflict, Equity shall prevail. At the same time it gave power to all the courts to administer the principles of Common Law and Equity and to grant the remedies of both, as circumstances in a case demanded. Consequently the old conflict no longer arises, although Common Law and Equity principles still exist.

By bringing the two systems together administratively, and allowing the High Court judge to exercise the principles, procedures and remedies of Common Law and Equity in a single case in the one court, it seemed to many people that the two systems had merged. That this was somewhat superficial is borne out by the exclusive jurisdictions left to the Queen's Bench and Chancery Divisions. In practice the work formerly done by the Court of Chancery is exactly that dealt with in the Chancery Division; equally it has its own judges selected from those barristers practising at the Chancery bar.

A Chancery case remains something quite unlike a Common Law case, and the same can be said of the procedure.

The whole of the legislation has now been consolidated in the Supreme Court Act 1981.

Probate, Divorce and Admiralty Jurisdiction

The Judicature Acts 1873–1875 in their reconstruction of the court system established a separate Division of the High Court of Justice called the Probate, Divorce and Admiralty Division. Why was it that these three branches of the law merited a Division of their own?

The answer is that these three important legal topics fell neither within the Common Law nor Equity jurisdictions, since Probate (which is concerned with wills) and Divorce were, for centuries, treated as ecclesiastical matters, and there was a separate Admiralty Court inevitably influenced by international shipping practices.

Probate and Divorce were transferred from the ecclesiastical courts to the ordinary civil courts in 1857 by the setting up of a Court of Probate and a separate Divorce Court.

The High Court of Admiralty although of great age historically gradually lost its widest jurisdiction to the Common Law courts, but it retained powers over collisions at sea, salvage and prize cases. All other aspects of the Law Merchant, that is the law affecting traders, had over the centuries been transferred to the Common Law courts.

Appeal Courts

The Judicature Acts 1873–1875 in creating a Court of Appeal alongside the new High Court of Justice had intended that this court with its specially designated Lords Justices of Appeal should be the final appellate court for civil matters. However, political considerations intervened and the proposal to remove judicial functions from the House of Lords was shelved. The Appellate Jurisdiction Act 1876 provided for the retention of the House of Lords as the final appeal court in civil cases and for the creation of special judges, Lords of Appeal in Ordinary, as life peers to staff the court.

6. Twentieth Century Developments

Criminal Courts

In 1907 the Criminal Appeal Act established the Court of Criminal Appeal to provide for the first time a general right of appeal for persons convicted and sentenced in indictable criminal cases. A further appeal in matters of general public importance lay to the

House of Lords. The Court of Criminal Appeal became the Court of Appeal (Criminal division) by the Criminal Appeal Act 1966.

The role of the Queen's Bench Divisional Court in ruling on points of law arising by way of case stated in summary criminal cases was amended by the Administration of Justice Act 1960. This Act enabled an appeal in a case of general public importance to be taken to the House of Lords if the divisional court grants a certificate to that effect and leave is obtained from the divisional court or the appeal committee of the House of Lords.

The court structure for trying indictable criminal cases was substantially changed by the Courts Act 1971 which abolished the historically derived Courts of Quarter Sessions and Assizes and replaced them with a court called the Crown Court. The Crown Court was to be organised on a six circuit basis so as to achieve a much needed flexibility to lead to the prompt trial of indictable criminal cases (and High Court civil actions too).

Civil Courts

The Administration of Justice Act 1970 created a Family Division of the High Court and amended the jurisdiction of the Queen's Bench and Chancery divisions redistributing the functions of the former Probate Divorce and Admiralty Division. One novel change in appeal provisions was the introduction by the Administration of Justice Act 1969 of a possible "leap-frog" appeal from the High Court to the House of Lords, by-passing the Court of Appeal. However, the procedure was made subject to stringent conditions which in practice limit its use (see p. 46).

15. The Changing Legal System

1. The Inevitability of Change

The one certainty in the study of any legal system is that it will be characterised by change. Pressure placed by the public on the politicians will lead to the legislature constantly producing new legislation. As all legislation involves new law every branch of the law, together with the legal system which lies behind it, is constantly undergoing change. Annually Parliament enacts some 80 new Acts of Parliament whilst substantial changes in existing law are also effected by the 2,000 new statutory instruments which become law every year.

Equally the decisions of the courts lead to significant changes in the law. There are today more judges, and more cases to be tried, then ever before. The judgments pronounced by the judges, and particularly those in the Court of Appeal and the House of Lords, involve the development of the legal principles in every branch of the law. As was seen in Chapter 11 the doctrine of judicial precedent is of particular importance in the English legal system. This is because the decisions of the judges make a continuous contribution to the growth of the various branches of the law. At the same time the obligation to strive for certainty and consistency causes the judge to ensure that his decision matches, derives from and supports the earlier decisions in that branch of the law.

Inevitably the more complex the society, the more complex the law and the more complicated the cases which arise. The student of contract will have observed how the nineteenth century leading cases concerned with the sale of horses have given way to involved transactions between large commercial corporations. Modern cases have found the courts concerned with, for example, the principles of offer and acceptance, when telex machines have been the channel of communication between the parties. As such cases are resolved so they add something to the previously accepted law in the law of con-

tract. The same is true of decisions in other branches of the law.
When it is recollected that every year many volumes of law reports
are published and that even so these contain only a fraction of the
total number of cases decided, the scale of change is self-evident.

The result is that in the modern state there can be no lull in legislation nor in case decisions, and the task of the lawyer in keeping
pace with change is unenviable, albeit fascinating. It might be
thought that changes in the system would be markedly fewer than
changes in substantive law, but in practice there is substantial and
constant pressure by pressure groups like Justice, the National
Council for Civil Liberties, the Howard League for Penal Reform,
the Statute Law Reform Society and the Legal Action Group, for
changes in the legal system. These changes may relate to criminal
procedure, to evidence, to the form of legislation or to such matters
as legal aid and advice.

2. Methods of Law Reform

Parliament

It is necessary that the methods by which changes in the law are
brought about should be examined. In the realm of change by legislation it is usually the case that the Act in question will have ema-
nated from the government department responsible for the matter,
probably at the request of the Minister for the time being. He, in
turn, will be under pressure from his Government colleagues.
Health legislation, for example, will be introduced by the Secretary
of State for the Social Services and will have been prepared initially
by his department. Only a very few private Members of Parliament
succeed each year in getting a public Act on to the Statute Book.
This is because parliamentary time is so valuable that the Government tends to demand almost all of it. If the production of legislation
by the government departments is examined, it will be apparent that
often the pressure for the legislation has come from interested bodies
outside Parliament who wish to see certain changes made. Some of
these pressure groups, like the National Farmers' Union or the
County Councils' Association, are very powerful organisations with
wide national support, but sometimes pressure from a small organisation can have the desired effect.

Very often legislation will be introduced following the report of a
Royal Commission or an ad hoc committee of inquiry. For example,
the report of the Widdicombe Committee Inquiry into the Conduct
of Local Authority Business was followed by the Local Government
Act 1986. Part II of that Act gave legislative force to the Widdicombe Committee recommendations.

The Judiciary

As was seen in Chapter 2 above the judicial function inevitably involves the creation of new law. However, the scope for the judge effectively to change the law is limited since the judge is presumed to be stating the principle of law which applies to the case, not himself producing a new principle of law. Equally important is the restraint imposed on the judge by the application of the doctrine of judicial precedent. Today it is rare for a case to arise for determination which involves an issue for which there is no precedent in point. Much more likely is the judicial difficulty of a plethora of conflicting authorities which the judge has to attempt to rationalise in his judgment.

Ostensibly judges are not concerned with law reform but it is not uncommon for them to draw attention to anomalies and to call for change. In *President of India* v. *La Pintada Compania* (1985) Lords Scarman and Roskill called for legislation to amend the law that interest cannot be charged on a debt paid late.

Advisory committees

For ensuring that improvements are made in the law as circumstances demand, certain standing committees have been set up with responsibility for reporting on particular matters in need of reform.

1. A Law Reform Committee, known originally as the Law Revision Committee, is appointed by the Lord Chancellor with the following terms of reference: "to consider, having regard especially to judicial decisions, what changes are desirable in such legal doctrines as the Lord Chancellor may from time to time refer to the committee." Membership of the committee, which is part-time, is made up of five judges, four practising barristers, two solicitors and three academic lawyers. Being part-time the meetings of the committee are occasional and although their reports have been very thorough, their total contribution to reform is limited. The committee is limited to civil matters and its reports have led to such legislation as the Occupiers' Liability Act 1957.

2. The Private International Law Committee was set up in 1952 as a standing body to advise the Lord Chancellor on matters of private international law and to assist in the holding of international conferences. At the present time it appears not to be operating.

3. The Criminal Law Revision Committee is the youngest of the advisory bodies having been established in 1959 to advise the Home Secretary. Its terms of reference are: "to examine such aspects of the criminal law of England and Wales as the Home Secretary may from time to time refer to the committee to consider whether the law

requires revision and to make recommendations." In composition it is very like the Law Reform Committee. It has produced on average one report a year; again it is a part-time body, and these reports have led to such legislation as the Suicide Act 1961 and the Theft Act 1968.

The Law Commission

The Labour Administration, which took office in 1964, passed, as a matter of urgency, the Law Commissions Act 1965 bringing into existence a body made up of five commissioners and a consultant, together with a staff of civil servants. This organisation gives its full time to law reform; in fact the exact terms of reference of the two commissions, one for England and Wales and one for Scotland, are "to keep under review all the law with which they are respectively concerned with a view to its systematic development and reform, including in particular the codification of such law, the elimination of anomalies, the repeal of obsolete and unnecessary enactments, the reduction of the number of separate enactments and generally the simplification and modernisation of the law."

The commissioners who have been appointed since 1965 have all been distinguished lawyers seconded from their employment for a five year period. The first chairman was a High Court judge, now Lord Scarman, and the present Chairman is Mr. Justice Beldam. The other commissioners have been either barristers or solicitors, and despite criticism, no lay representatives have been given the opportunity to become commissioners. It is comparatively early to attempt to assess the effect of the Law Commission on its vast task, but a large number of recommendations from its many Reports have found their way into legislation. The annual report of the Law Commission contains an appendix which shows whether or not its Reports have been given effect. Until recently implementation by legislation has been quick and effective but the more recent reports have complained of a slowing down in the Government's announcement of its policy towards the Commission's and other law reform bodies' recommendations. The Land Registration Act 1986, for instance, implements a 1983 report of the Law Commission.

The 1965 Act, as well as giving the Law Commission major responsibilities for law reform, specified, it will be noted, four separate features which that body is to have regard to in the course of its work. These are codification of law, the repeal of obsolete and unnecessary enactments, the reduction of the number of separate enactments and the elimination of anomalies. Codification is inevitably a long-term plan. Since in each case the ultimate objective is a single self-contained code, which will be "the statement of all the relevant law in a logical and coherent form." Good progress has been made in the repeal of obsolete statutory provisions, in particular by the enactment of several Statute Law (Repeals) Acts, the latest being in 1986, and in the passage of many consolidating statutes which contribute to a simplification of the law.

In the White Paper published by the Labour Government in advance of the introduction of the Law Commissions Bill the point was made that there was an urgent need for a review body. This was substantiated by the fact that there was said to exist some 3,000 Acts of Parliament dating from 1234, many volumes of delegated legislation and some 300,000 reported case decisions. Looked at in this light, the Law Commission deserves to remain a permanent institution in the English legal system.

Consolidation and codification

The work of the Law Commission leads on to a consideration of the actual process by which legislation is simplified. Under the Consolidation of Enactments (Procedure) Act 1949 a system was introduced by Parliament under which, where the bringing together of separate statutory provisions, known as "consolidation," was deemed to be desirable, the Lord Chancellor could arrange to have prepared a memorandum showing how these various provisions would take effect in the proposed consolidating Act. Thus, for example, the whole of the legislation concerned with county courts was brought together in the County Courts Act 1984. The memorandum is duly placed before a joint committee of both Houses of Parliament. If this joint committee approves the proposed consolidating measure, it is virtually certain to be passed by both Houses without the need for lengthy debates. Since the Bill is little more than a simplifying measure the examination by the joint committee is generally acceptable to the members of both Houses.

This procedure is not possible where the Bill involves changes of substance in the law, known as "codification." A codifying measure brings together the existing statute and case law, in an attempt to produce a full statement as it relates to that particular branch of law. The main examples of successful codification date from the end of the nineteenth century when the following four statutes were passed: the Bills of Exchange Act 1882, the Partnership Act 1890, the Sale of Goods Act 1893 and the Marine Insurance Act 1906. The Bills of Exchange Act 1882, which was prepared by Sir M. D. Chalmers, involved the consideration of 17 existing statutes and some 2,500 decided cases. These were compressed to make a statute 100 sections long. After these Acts were passed, there was no more codifying legislation until the Theft Act 1968.

Today there is considerable talk of the introduction of codifying statutes, so that the coming decade may witness new examples of this type of legislation. The Law Commission has recently published a suggested codification of Criminal Law. A major consideration is the question of parliamentary time. Unlike a consolidating measure, the fact that a codifying Bill proposes to change the law means that Members of Parliament will wish to debate it.

3. Change and the English Legal System

Just as the 1970's proved to be an important decade for changes in the English legal system (see the Third Edition) so the 1980's seem set to increase the pace of change.

Major consolidating legislation has affected the magistrates courts (Magistrates Courts Act 1980) the county court (County Courts Act 1984) and the supreme court (Supreme Court Act 1981).

Procedure in the courts has been and continues to be the subject of close scrutiny. Currently consultants and an independent advisory committee with the Lord Chancellor are reviewing civil procedure with the object of reducing delay, cost and complexity. To this end changes may be expected in jurisdiction, procedure and court administration. In the criminal law sphere the report of the Royal Commission on Criminal Procedure has led to important changes in sentencing policy in the Criminal Justice Act 1982, and to major legislation on police powers, civil liberties and the law relating to evidence in criminal cases. The ramifications of the Police and Criminal Evidence Act 1984 and the Public Order Act 1986, have yet to be fully felt. A notable amendment to the Legal Aid scheme, in the Legal Aid Act 1982, has led to the establishment of a duty solicitor scheme for magistrates courts. Of equal consequence is the establishment of the Crown Prosecution Service to take over from the police the responsibility for prosecuting offenders as laid down in the Prosecution of Offences Act 1985.

The future of the legal profession is very much in question at the time of writing. The Administration of Justice Act 1985 has taken away the solicitors' monopoly in conveyancing: with the predictable result that many of the longstanding restrictive practices of both the barrister and the solicitor are being questioned. Even such delicate subjects as judicial appointments, training and dismissal are under consideration with widespread pressure for change.

Problems arising from the increasing cost of legal aid to the public purse have led to litigation between the legal profession and the

Lord Chancellor (1986) and the spectacle of the Lord Chancellor's Department suggesting radical changes in the legal aid fee arrangements—for example, counsel appearing without solicitor, and Queen's Counsel appearing without junior counsel—solely to save money. Equally disturbing are other proposals to change, for example, the eight-day maximum remand in custody provision, the existing system of committal proceedings and also to remove, perhaps to Citizens' Advice Bureaux, the legal advice and assistance scheme now operated by solicitors.

Further Reading

For further reading and detailed references the following texts and reports are recommended:

R. J. Walker: *Walker and Walker: The English Legal System* (6th ed., 1985) (Butterworths)

M. Zander: *Cases and Materials on the English Legal System* (4th ed., Weidenfeld and Nicolson 1984

P. F. Smith and S. H. Bailey: *The Modern English Legal System* (1984) (Sweet and Maxwell)

R. White: *The administration of Justice* (1985) (Blackwell)

The Legal Profession

The Royal Commission on Legal Services Report, Cmnd 7648 (1979)

R.L. Abel: *The decline of professionalism* [1986] M.L.R.1.

Judges

S. Shetreet: *Judges on Trial* (1976) (North Holland Publishing Company)

J. A. G. Griffith: *The Politics of the Judiciary* (3rd ed., 1985) (Collins)

Magistrates

Sir T. Skyrme: *The Changing Image of the Magistracy* (2nd ed., 1983) (Macmillan)

The Jury

Lord Devlin: *Trial by Jury* (1966) (Hamlyn Lextures)

W. R. Cornish: *The Jury* (1968) (Allen Lane)

N. Walker ed: *The British Jury System* (1975) (C.U.P.)

J. Baldwin and M. McConville: *Jury Trials* (1979) (O.U.P.)

The Courts

L. Blom Cooper and G. Drewry: *Final Appeal* (1972) (O.U.P.)
Annual Judicial Statistics: Lord Chancellor's Department
M. Furmston et al: *The effect on English Domestic Law of Membership of the European Communities and of ratification of the European Convention on Human Rights* (1983) (The Hague)

Procedure and Evidence

D. Barnard: *The Civil Court in Action.* (2nd ed., 1985) (Butterworths)
D. Barnard: The Criminal Court in Action. (3rd ed., 1986) (Butterworths)

Tribunals, Inquiries and Arbitration

Annual Reports of the Council on Tribunals.

Legal Aid and Advice

Annual Reports of the Lord Chancellor's Legal Aid Advisory Committee.

Sources

Sir A. R. N. Cross: *Precedent in English Law* (3rd ed., 1977) (O.U.P.)
Statutory Interpretation (1976) (O.U.P.)
M. Zander: *The Law Making Process.* (1980) (Weidenfeld and Nicolson)

History

J. H. Baker: *Introduction to English Legal History* (2nd ed., 1979) (Butterworths)

The Changing Legal System

Annual Reports of the Law Commission.

Index